VAILIMA LETTERS

VAILIMA LETTERS

BEING CORRESPONDENCE

ADDRESSED BY

ROBERT LOUIS STEVENSON

TO

SIDNEY COLVIN

NOVEMBER, 1890—OCTOBER, 1894

IN TWO VOLUMES

VOL. I.

GREENWOOD PRESS, PUBLISHERS
NEW YORK

Originally published in 1895
by Stone & Kimball

First Greenwood Reprinting 1969

Library of Congress Catalogue Card Number 69-14102

SBN 8371-1625-2

PRINTED IN UNITED STATES OF AMERICA

CONTENTS.

VOL. I.

*The Frontispiece is a portrait of R. L. Stevenson etched by
W. Strang after a photograph by Falk, of Sydney.*

EDITORIAL NOTE.

So much of preface seems necessary to this volume as may justify its publication and explain its origin. The writer was for many years my closest friend. It was in the summer of 1873 that a lady, whose gracious influence has helped to shape and encourage more than one distinguished career, first awakened my interest in him and drew us together. He was at that time a lad of twenty-two, with his powers not yet set nor his way of life determined. But to know him was to recognize at once that here was a young genius of whom great things might be expected. A slender, boyish presence, with a graceful, somewhat fantastic bearing, and a singular power and attraction in the eyes and smile, were the signs that first impressed you; and the impression was quickly confirmed and deepened by the charm of his talk, which was irresistibly sympathetic and inspiring, and not less full of matter than of mirth. I have known no man in whom the poet's heart and imagination were combined with such a brilliant strain of humor and such an unsleeping alertness and adroitness of the critical intelligence. But it was only in conversation that he could as yet do himself justice. His earliest efforts in literature were of a very uneven and tentative quality. The reason partly was that in mode of expression and choice of language, not less than in the formation of opinion and the conduct of life, he was impatient, even to excess, of the conventional, the accepted, and the trite. His perceptions and emotions were acute and vivid in the extreme; his judgments, whether founded on experience, reading, discussion, or caprice (and a surprising amount of all these things had been crowded into his youthful existence) were not less fresh and personal; while to his ardent fancy the world was a theatre glowing with the lights and bustling with the incidents of romance. To find for all he had to say words of vital aptness and animation — to communicate as much as possible of what he has somewhere called "the incommunicable thrill of things" — was from the first his endeavor in literature, — nay more, it was the main passion of his life. The instrument that should serve his purpose could not be forged in haste, still less could it be adopted at second hand or ready made; and he has himself narrated how long and toilsome was the apprentice-ship he served.

In those days, then, of Stevenson's youth it was my good fortune to be of use to him, partly by helping to soften paren-tal opposition to his inborn vocation for letters, partly by recommending him to editors (Mr. Hamerton, Sir George Grove, and Mr. Leslie Stephen in succession), and a little even by such technical hints as a classical training and five years' senior-

ity enabled me to give. It belonged to
the richness of his nature to repay in all
things much for little, ἑκατόμβοι' ἐννεαβοίων,
and from these early relations sprang both
the affection, to me inestimable, of which
the following correspondence bears evidence, and the habit, which it pleased him
to maintain after he had become one of the
acknowledged masters of English letters,
of confiding in and consulting me about
his work in progress. It was my business
to find fault; to "damn" what I did not
like; a duty which, as will be inferred
from the following pages, I was accustomed
to discharge somewhat unsparingly. But
he was too manly a spirit to desire or to
relish flattery, and too true an artist to be
content with doing less than his best: he
knew, moreover, in what rank of English
writers I put him, and for what audience,
not of to-day, I would have him labor.
Tibi Palinure — so, in the last weeks of
his life, he proposed to inscribe to me a
set of his collected works. Not Palinurus

so much as Polonius may perhaps — or so
I sometimes suspect — have been really
the character; but his own amiable view of
the matter has to be mentioned in order to
account for part of the tenor of the following correspondence.

As a letter-writer, Mr. Stevenson was
punctilious in business matters (herein
putting some violence on his nature), indefatigable where there was a service to
be requited or a kindness done, and to
strangers and slight acquaintances ever
courteous and attentive. I am not sure,
indeed, but that in this capacity it was the
outer and not the inner circle of his corre-
spondents who, speaking generally, had
the best of him. To his intimate friends
he wrote charmingly indeed by fits, but
often, at least in early days, in a manner
not a little trying and tantalizing. With
these, his correspondence was apt to be a
thing wholly of moods. "Sordid facts," as
he called them, were almost never mentioned: date and place one could never

infer except from the postmark.   He would
exclaim over some predicament to the
nature of which he gave no clue whatever,
or appeal for sympathy in circumstances
impossible to conjecture; or, starting in a
key of vague poetry and sentiment, would
wind up (in a manner characteristic also of
his talk) with a rhapsody of hyperbolical
slang.   Or he would dilate on some new
phase of his many maladies with burlesque
humor, — with complaint never; but what
had been the nature of the attack you were
left to wonder and guess in vain.   During
the period of his Odyssey in the South
Seas, from August, 1888, until the spring
of 1890, the remoteness and inaccessibility
of the scenes he visited inevitably interrupted all correspondence for months
together; and when at long intervals a
packet reached us, the facts and circumstances of his wanderings were to be
gathered from the admirable letters of Mrs.
Stevenson (who has this feminine accom-
plishment in perfection) rather than from

his own. But when later in the last-
mentioned year 1890, he and his family
were settled on their newly bought property
on the mountain behind Apia, to which he
gave the name of Vailima (five rivers), he
for the first time, to my infinite gratifica-
tion, took to writing me long and regular
monthly budgets as full and particular as
heart could wish; and this practice he
maintained until within a few weeks of his
death.

It is these journal-letters from Samoa,
covering with a few intervals the period
from November, 1890, to October, 1894,
that are printed by themselves in the
present volume. They occupy a place, as
has been indicated, quite apart in his correspondence, and in any general selection
from his letters would fill a quite dispro-
portionate space. Begun without a thought
of publicity, and simply to maintain our
intimacy undiminished, so far as might be,
by separation, they assumed in the course
of two or three years a bulk so consider-

able, and contained so much of the matter
of his daily life and thoughts, that it by and
by occurred to him, as may be read on page
38 of vol. ii., that "some kind of a book"
might be extracted out of them after his
death. It is this passage which has given
me my warrant for their publication, and at
the same time has imposed on me no very
easy editorial task. In a correspondence
so unreserved, the duty of suppression and
selection must needs be delicate. Belong-
ing to the race of Scott and Dumas, of the
romantic narrators and creators, Stevenson
belonged no less to that of Montaigne and
the literary egotists. The word seems out
of place, since of egotism in the sense of
vanity or selfishness he was of all men the
most devoid; but he was nevertheless a
watchful and ever interested observer of
the motions of his own mind. He saw
himself, as he saw everything else (to
borrow the words of Mr. Andrew Lang),
with the lucidity of genius, and loved to
put himself on terms of confidence with

his readers; but of confidence kept always within fit limits, and permitting no undue intrusion into his private affairs and feelings. To maintain the same limits in the editing of an intimate correspondence after his death would have been impossible. I have tried to do my best under the circumstances; to suffer no feelings to be hurt that could be spared, and only to lift the veil of family life so far as under the conditions was unavoidable. Neither would it have been possible from such a correspondence to expunge the record of those trivialities which make up the chief part of life, even in surroundings so romantic and unusual as Stevenson in these years had chosen for himself. It belonged to the personal charm of the man that nothing ever seemed commonplace or insignificant in his company; but in correspondence this charm must needs to some extent evaporate.

Such as they remain, then, these letters will be found a varied record, perfectly

frank and familiar, of the writer's every-
day moods, thoughts, and doings during
his Samoan exile. They tell, with the
zest and often in the language of a man
who remained to the last a boy in spirit,
of the pleasures and troubles of a planter
founding his home in the virgin soil of
a tropical island; the pleasures of an in-
valid beginning after many years to resume habits of outdoor life and exercise;
the toils and satisfactions, failures and
successes, of a creative artist whose inven-
tion was as fertile as his standards were
high and his industry unflinching. These
divers characters have probably never been
so united in any man before. Something
also they tell of the inward movements
and affections of one of the bravest and
tenderest of human hearts. One part of
his life, it should be said, which his other
letters will fully reveal, finds little expression in these, namely, the relations of cor-
dial and ungrudging kindness in which he
stood towards the younger generation of

writers at home, including those person-
ally unknown to him.   Neither do ordinary
impressions of travel, — impressions of the
beauties of the tropics and the capitivating
strangeness of the island people and their
ways, — fill much space in them.   These
things were no longer new to the writer
when the correspondence began; they had
been part of the element of his life since
the day, near two years before, when his
yacht first anchored in the Bay of Nukahiva,
and his soul, to quote his own words,
"went down with these moorings whence
no windlass may extract nor any diver fish
it up; and I, and some part of my ship's
company, were from that hour the bond-
slaves of the isles of Vivien."   In their
stead we find, what to some readers may be
hardly so welcome, the observations of a
close student of native life, history, and
manners, and some of the perplexities and
preoccupations of an island politician.

The political allusions are seldom in the
form of direct statement or narrative.   To

understand them, the reader must bear in mind a few main facts, which I shall state as briefly and plainly as possible. At the date when Stevenson settled in Samoa, the government of the island had lately been settled between the three powers interested, namely, Germany, England, and the United States, at the convention of Berlin. Under this convention, Malietoa Laupepa, who had previously been deposed and deported by the Germans in favor of a nominee of their own, was reinstated as king, to the exclusion of his kinsman, the powerful and popular Mataafa, whose titles might be held equally good, and whose abilities were certainly greater, but who was specially obnoxious to the Germans, owing to his resistance to them during the troubles of the previous years. For a time, the two kinsmen, Laupepa and Mataafa, lived on amicable terms; but presently differences arose between them. Mataafa had expected to occupy a position of influence in the government; finding himself ignored, he withdrew to a camp a few miles outside the town of Apia, where he lived in semi-royal state as a kind of passive rebel or rival to the recognized king. In the mean time, in the course of the year 1891, the two white officials appointed under the Berlin Convention, namely, the Chief Justice, a Swedish gentleman named Cedarkrantz, and the President of the Council, Baron Senfft von Pilsach, had come out to the islands and entered on their duties. In Stevenson's judgment these gentlemen proved quite unequal to their task, — an opinion which before long came to be shared and acted on by the Foreign Offices of the three powers under whom they were appointed. Stevenson was no abstracted student or dreamer; the human interests and the human duties lying immediately about him were ever the first in his eyes; and, petty and remote as these island concerns may appear to us, they were for him near and urgent. A man of his eager nature and persuasive

powers must naturally acquire influence in
any community in which he may be thrown,
and among the natives in especial by kindness, justice, and a sympathetic understand-
ing of their ways and characters he soon
came to enjoy a singular degree of authority.
His unauthorized intervention in public
matters may have been of a nature dis-
concerting to the official mind, but his
purposes were at all times those of a
peacemaker. The steady aim of his efforts
was to bring about the withdrawal of the
two discredited white officials (against
whom, it will be seen, he had no personal
animus whatever) and to procure a recon-
ciliation between Laupepa and Mataafa,
so that the latter might exercise the share
in the government due to his character,
titles, and following. The first part of
this policy commended itself after a time to
the three powers and their agents, and was
carried out; the second not; and his friend
Mataafa was by and by attacked by the forces
of Laupepa, beaten, and sent into exile.

In reading the following pages it must be borne in mind that Mulinuu and Malie, the places respectively of Laupepa's and Mataafa's residence, are also used to signify their respective parties and followings. The reader will have no difficulty in identifying the various personages composing the family group whose names occur constantly in the correspondence, namely, the writer's mother, his wife ("Fanny"), his stepson, Mr. Lloyd Osbourne ("Lloyd"), his step-daughter and amanuensis, Mrs. Strong ("Belle"), and her young son ("Austin"). Explanation of any other matters seeming to require it is added in the footnotes.

S. C.

August, 1895.

I

In the Mountain, Apia, Samoa,
Monday, November 2d, 1890.

MY DEAR COLVIN, — This is a hard and
interesting and beautiful life that we lead
now.   Our place is in a deep cleft of Vaea
Mountain, some six hundred feet above the
sea, embowered in forest, which is our
strangling enemy, and which we combat
with axes and dollars.   I went crazy over
outdoor work, and had at last to confine
myself to the house, or literature must
have gone by the board.   *Nothing* is so
interesting as weeding, clearing, and path-
making; the oversight of laborers becomes
a disease; it is quite an effort not to drop
into the farmer; and it does make you feel
so well.   To come down covered with
mud and drenched with sweat and rain
after some hours in the bush, change, rub
down, and take a chair in the veranda, is

to taste a quiet conscience. And the
strange thing that I mark is this: If I
go out and make sixpence, bossing my
labourers and plying the cutlass or the
spade, idiot conscience applauds me; if I
sit in the house and make twenty pounds,
idiot conscience wails over my neglect and
the day wasted. For near a fortnight I
did not go beyond the verandah; then I
found my rush of work run out, and went
down for the night to Apia; put in Sunday
afternoon with our consul, "a nice young
man," dined with my friend H. J. Moors in
the evening, went to church — no less — at
the white and half-white church — I had
never been before, and was much interested; the woman I sat next *looked* a full-
blood native, and it was in the prettiest
and readiest English that she sang the
hymns; back to Moors', where we yarned
of the islands, being both wide wanderers,
till bed-time; bed, sleep, breakfast, horse
saddled; round to the mission, to get Mr.
Clarke to be my interpreter; over with

him to the King's, whom I have not called
on since my return; received by that mild
old gentleman; have some interesting talk
with him about Samoan superstitions and
my land — the scene of a great battle in
his (Malietoa Laupepa's) youth — the place
which we have cleared the platform of his
fort — the gulley of the stream full of dead
bodies — the fight rolled off up Vaea
mountain-side; back with Clarke to the
Mission; had a bit of lunch and consulted
over a queer point of missionary policy
just arisen, about our new Town Hall and
the balls there — too long to go into, but a
quaint example of the intricate questions
which spring up daily in the missionary
path.[1]

[1] " In the missionary work which is being done among
the Samoans, Mr. Stevenson was especially interested.
He was an observant, shrewd, yet ever generous critic
of all our religious and educational organisations. His
knowledge of native character and life enabled him to
understand missionary difficulties, while his genial con-
tact with all sorts and conditions of men made him keen
to detect deficiencies in men and methods, and apt in
useful suggestion." The above is the testimony of the

Then off up the hill; Jack very fresh, the sun (close on noon) staring hot, the breeze very strong and pleasant; the ineffable green country all round — gorgeous little birds (I think they are humming-birds, but they say not) skirmishing in the wayside flowers. About a quarter way up I met a native coming down with the trunk of a cocoa palm across his shoulder; his brown breast glittering with sweat and oil: "Talofa" — "Talofa, alii — You see that white man? He speak for you." "White man he gone up here?" — " Ioe (Yes) " — "Tofa, alii" — "Tofa, soifua!" I put on Jack up the steep path, till he is all as white as shaving stick — Brown's euxesis, wish I had some — past Tanugamanono, a bush village — see into the houses as I pass — they are open sheds scattered on a green — see the brown folk sitting there,

Mr. Clarke here mentioned (Rev. W. E. Clarke of the London Missionary Society). This gentleman was from the first one of the most valued friends of Mr. Stevenson and his family in Samoa, and when the end came, read the funeral service beside his grave on Mount Vaea.

suckling kids, sleeping on their stiff wooden pillows — then on through the wood path — and here I find the mysterious white man (poor devil!) with his twenty years' certificate of good behaviour as a book-keeper, frozen out by the strikes in the colonies, come up here on a chance, no work to be found, big hotel bill, no ship to leave in — and come up to beg twenty dollars because he heard I was a Scotch-man, offering to leave his portmanteau in pledge. Settle this, and on again; and here my house comes in view, and a war whoop fetches my wife and Henry (or Simelé), our Samoan boy, on the front balcony; and I am home again, and only sorry that I shall have to go down again to Apia this day week. I could, and would, dwell here unmoved, but there are things to be attended to.

Never say I don't give you details and news. That is a picture of a letter.

I have been hard at work since I came; three chapters of *The Wrecker*, and since

that, eight of the South Sea book, and
along and about and in between, a hatful of
verses. Some day I 'll send the verse to
you, and you 'll say if any of it is any
good. I have got in a better vein with the
South Sea book, as I think you will see;
I think these chapters will do for the
volume without much change. Those that
I did in the *Janet Nicoll*, under the most
ungodly circumstances, I fear will want a
lot of suppling and lightening, but I hope
to have your remarks in a month or two
upon that point. It seems a long while
since I have heard from you. I do hope
you are well. I am wonderful, but tired
from so much work; 't is really immense
what I have done; in the South Sea book
I have fifty pages copied fair, some of
which has been four times, and all twice
written; certainly fifty pages of solid scriv-
ing inside a fortnight, but I was at it by
seven A. M. till lunch, and from two till
four or five every day; between whiles,
verse and blowing on the flageolet; never

outside. If you could see this place! but
I don't want any one to see it till my
clearing is done, and my house built. It
will be a home for angels.

So far I wrote after my bit of dinner,
some cold meat and bananas, on arrival.
Then out to see where Henry and some of
the men were clearing the garden; for it
was plain there was to be no work to-day
indoors, and I must set in consequence to
farmering. I stuck a good while on the
way up, for the path there is largely my
own handiwork, and there were a lot of
sprouts and saplings and stones to be
removed. Then I reached our clearing
just where the streams join in one; it had
a fine autumn smell of burning, the smoke
blew in the woods, and the boys were
pretty merry and busy. Now I had a
private design: —

The Vaita'e I had explored pretty far
up; not yet the other stream, the Vaituliga
(g = nasal n, as ng in sing); and up that,
with my wood knife, I set off alone. It is

1890
Nov.
here quite dry; it went through endless
woods; about as broad as a Devonshire
lane, here and there crossed by fallen
trees; huge trees overhead in the sun,
dripping lianas and tufted with orchids,
tree ferns, ferns depending with air roots
from the steep banks, great arums — I had

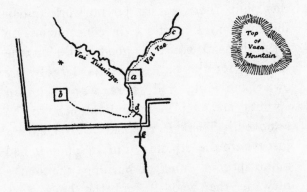

not skill enough to say if any of them were
the edible kind, one of our staples here!
— hundreds of bananas — another staple —
and alas! I had skill enough to know all
of these for the bad kind that bears no
fruit. My Henry moralised over this the

other day; how hard it was that the bad banana flourished wild, and the good must be weeded and tended; and I had not the heart to tell him how fortunate they were here, and how hungry were other lands by comparison. The ascent of this lovely lane of my dry stream filled me with delight. I could not but be reminded of old Mayne Reid, as I have been more than once since I came to the tropics; and I thought, if Reid had been still living, I would have written to tell him that, for me, *it had come true;* and I thought, forbye, that, if the great powers go on as they are going, and the Chief Justice delays, it would come truer still; and the war-conch will sound in the hills, and my home will be enclosed in camps, before the year is ended. And all at once — mark you, how Mayne Reid is on the spot — a strange thing happened. I saw a liana stretch across the bed of the brook about breast-high, swung up my knife to sever it, and — behold, it was a wire! On either hand it plunged into thick bush; to-morrow I shall see where it goes and get a guess perhaps of what it means. To-day I know no more than — there it is. A little higher the brook began to trickle, then to fill. At last, as I meant to do some work upon the homeward trail, it was time to turn. I did not return by the stream; knife in hand, as long as my endurance lasted, I was to cut a path in the congested bush.

At first it went ill with me; I got badly stung as high as the elbows by the stinging plant; I was nearly hung in a tough liana — a rotten trunk giving way under my feet; it was deplorable bad business. And an axe — if I dared swing one — would have been more to the purpose than my cutlass. Of a sudden things began to go strangely easier; I found stumps, bushing out again; my body began to wonder, then my mind; I raised my eyes and looked ahead; and, by George, I was no longer pioneering, I had struck an old

track overgrown, and was restoring an old
path.   So I laboured till I was in such a
state that Carolina Wilhelmina Skeggs
could scarce have found a name for it.
Thereon desisted; returned to the stream;
made my way down that stony track to the
garden, where the smoke was still hanging
and the sun was still in the high tree-tops,
and so home.   Here, fondly supposing my
long day was over, I rubbed down; exquisite agony; water spreads the poison of
these weeds; I got it all over my hands,
on my chest, in my eyes, and presently,
while eating an orange, *à la* Raratonga,
burned my lip and eye with orange juice.
Now, all day, our three small pigs had
been adrift, to the mortal peril of our
corn, lettuce, onions, etc., and as I stood
smarting on the back verandah, behold the
three piglings issuing from the wood just
opposite.   Instantly I got together as
many boys as I could — three, and got the
pigs penned against the rampart of the sty,
till the others joined; whereupon we

formed a cordon, closed, captured the deserters, and dropped them, squeaking amain, into their strengthened barracks where, please God, they may now stay!

Perhaps you may suppose the day now over; you are not the head of a plantation, my juvenile friend. Politics succeeded: Henry got adrift in his English, Bene was too cowardly to tell me what he was after: result, I have lost seven good labourers, and had to sit down and write to you to keep my temper. Let me sketch my lads. — Henry — Henry has gone down to town or I could not be writing to you — this were the hour of his English lesson else, when he learns what he calls "long explessions" or "your chief's language" for the matter of an hour and a half — Henry is a chiefling from Savaii; I once loathed, I now like and — pending fresh discoveries — have a kind of respect for Henry. He does good work for us; goes among the labourers, bossing and watching; helps Fanny; is civil, kindly, thoughtful; *O si*

sic semper! But will he be "his sometime
self throughout the year"? Anyway, he
has deserved of us, and he must disappoint
me sharply ere I give him up. — Bene — or
Peni — Ben, in plain English — is supposed
to be my ganger; the Lord love him! God
made a truckling coward, there is his full
history. He cannot tell me what he wants;
he dares not tell me what is wrong; he
dares not transmit my orders or translate
my censures. And with all this, honest,
sober, industrious, miserably smiling over
the miserable issue of his own unmanliness.
— Paul — a German — cook and steward
— a glutton of work — a splendid fellow;
drawbacks, three: (1) no cook; (2) an in-
veterate bungler; a man with twenty
thumbs, continually falling in the dishes,
throwing out the dinner, preserving the
garbage; (3) a dr—, well, don't let us say
that — but we dare n't let him go to town,
and he — poor, good soul — is afraid to be
let go. — Lafaele (Raphael), a strong, dull,
deprecatory man; splendid with an axe, if

watched; the better for a rowing, when he
calls me "Papa" in the most wheedling
tones; desperately afraid of ghosts, so that
he dare not walk alone up in the banana
patch — see map. The rest are changing
labourers; and to-night, owing to the miserable cowardice of Peni, who did not
venture to tell me what the men wanted —
and which was no more than fair — all are
gone — and my weeding in the article of
being finished! Pity the sorrows of a
planter.

I am, Sir, yours, and be jowned to you,
The Planter,   R. L. S.

Tuesday, 3rd.

I begin to see the whole scheme of
letter-writing; you sit down every day and
pour out an equable stream of twaddle.

This morning all my fears were fled, and
all the trouble had fallen to the lot of Peni
himself, who deserved it; my field was full
of weeders; and I am again able to justify
the ways of God. All morning I worked

at the South Seas, and finished the chapter I had stuck upon on Saturday. Fanny, awfully hove-to with rheumatics and injuries received upon the field of sport and glory, chasing pigs, was unable to go up and down stairs, so she sat upon the back verandah, and my work was chequered by her cries. "Paul, you take a spade to do that — dig a hole first. If you do that, you 'll cut your foot off! Here, you boy, what you do there? You no get work? You go find Simelé; he give you work. Peni, you tell this boy he go find Simelé; suppose Simelé no give him work, you tell him go 'way. I no want him here. That boy no good." — *Peni* (from the distance in reassuring tones), "All right, sir!"— *Fanny* (after a long pause), "Peni, you tell that boy go find Simelé! I no want him stand here all day. I no pay that boy. I see him all day. He no do nothing." — Luncheon, beef, soda-scones, fried bananas, pineapple in claret, coffee. Try to write a poem; no go. Play the flageolet. Then

sneakingly off to farmering and pioneering.
Four gangs at work on our place; a lively
scene; axes crashing and smoke blowing;
all the knives are out. But I rob the
garden party of one without a stock, and
you should see my hand — cut to ribbons.
Now I want to do my path up the Vaituliga
single-handed, and I want it to burst on
the public complete. Hence, with devilish
ingenuity, I begin it at different places;
so that if you stumble on one section, you
may not even then suspect the fulness of
my labours. Accordingly, I started in a
new place, below the wire, and hoping to
work up to it. It was perhaps lucky I had
so bad a cutlass, and my smarting hand bid
me stay before I had got up to the wire, but
just in season, so that I was only the better
of my activity, not dead beat as yesterday.

A strange business it was, and infinitely
solitary; away above, the sun was in the
high tree-tops; the lianas noosed and
sought to hang me; the saplings struggled,
and came up with that sob of death that

one gets to know so well; great, soft, sappy trees fell at a lick of the cutlass, little tough switches laughed at and dared my best endeavour. Soon, toiling down in that pit of verdure, I heard blows on the far side, and then laughter. I confess a chill settled on my heart. Being so dead alone, in a place where by rights none should be beyond me, I was aware, upon interrogation, if those blows had drawn nearer, I should (of course quite unaffectedly) have executed a strategic movement to the rear; and only the other day I was lamenting my insensibility to superstition! Am I beginning to be sucked in? Shall I become a midnight twitterer like my neighbours? At times I thought the blows were echoes; at times I thought the laughter was from birds. For our birds are strangely human in their calls. Vaea mountain about sundown sometimes rings with shrill cries, like the hails of merry, scattered children. As a matter of fact, I believe stealthy wood-cutters from Tanugamanono were above me in the wood and answerable for the blows; as for the laughter, a woman and two children had come and asked Fanny's leave to go up shrimp-fishing in the burn; beyond doubt, it was these I heard. Just at the right time I returned; to wash down, change, and begin this snatch of letter before dinner was ready, and to finish it afterwards, before Henry has yet put in an appearance for his lesson in "long explessions."

Dinner: stewed beef and potatoes, baked bananas, new loaf-bread hot from the oven, pineapple in claret. These are great days; we have been low in the past; but now are we as belly-gods, enjoying all things.

Wednesday. (*Hist. Vailima resumed.*)

A gorgeous evening of after-glow in the great tree-tops and behind the mountain, and full moon over the lowlands and the sea, inaugurated a night of horrid cold. To you effete denizens of the so-called temperate zone, it had seemed nothing; neither of us could sleep; we were up seeking extra coverings, I know not at what hour — it was as bright as day. The moon right over Vaea — near due west, the birds strangely silent, and the wood of the house tingling with cold; I believe it must have been 60°! Consequence; Fanny has a headache and is wretched, and I could do no work. (I am trying all round for a place to hold my pen; you will hear why later on; this to explain penmanship.) I wrote two pages, very bad, no movement, no life or interest; then I wrote a business letter; then took to tootling on the flageolet, till glory should call me farmering.

I took up at the fit time Lafaele and Maugà — Mauga, accent on the first, is a mountain, I don't know what Maugà means — mind what I told you of the value of g — to the garden, and set them digging, then turned my attention to the path. I could not go into my bush path for two reasons: 1st, sore hands; 2nd, had on my

trousers and good shoes. Lucky it was.
Right in the wild lime hedge which cuts
athwart us just homeward of the garden, I
found a great bed of kuikui — sensitive
plant — our deadliest enemy. A fool
brought it to this island in a pot, and used
to lecture and sentimentalise over the
tender thing. The tender thing has now
taken charge of this island, and men fight
it, with torn hands, for bread and life. A
singular, insidious thing, shrinking and
biting like a weasel; clutching by its roots
as a limpet clutches to a rock. As I fought
him, I bettered some verses in my poem,
the *Woodman;*[1] the only thought I gave
to letters. Though the kuikui was thick,
there was but a small patch of it, and
when I was done I attacked the wild lime,
and had a hand-to-hand skirmish with its
spines and elastic suckers. All this time,
close by, in the cleared space of the garden,
Lafaele and Maugà were digging. Suddenly quoth Lafaele, "Somebody he sing

[1] Published in the *New Review*, January, 1895.

out." — "Somebody he sing out? All
right. I go." And I went and found
they had been whistling and "singing out"
for long, but the fold of the hill and the
uncleared bush shuts in the garden so that
no one heard, and I was late for dinner,
and Fanny's headache was cross; and when
the meal was over, we had to cut up a
pineapple which was going bad, to make
jelly of; and the next time you have a
handful of broken blood-blisters, apply
pineapple juice, and you will give me news
of it, and I request a specimen of your
hand of write five minutes after — the
historic moment when I tackled this
history. My day so far.

Fanny was to have rested. Blessed Paul
began making a duck-house; she let him
be; the duck-house fell down, and she had
to set her hand to it. He was then to
make a drinking-place for the pigs; she let
him be again — he made a stair by which
the pigs will probably escape this evening,
and she was near weeping. Impossible to

1890
Nov.

blame the indefatigable fellow; energy is too rare and good-will too noble a thing to discourage; but it's trying when she wants a rest. Then she had to cook the dinner; then, of course — like a fool and a woman — must wait dinner for me, and make a flurry of herself. Her day so far. *Cetera adhunc desunt.*

Friday — I think.

I have been too tired to add to this chronicle, which will at any rate give you some guess of our employment. All goes well; the kuikui — (think of this mispronunciation having actually infected me to the extent of misspelling! tuitui is the word by rights) — the tuitui is all out of the paddock — a fenced park between the house and boundary; Peni's men start to-day on the road; the garden is part burned, part dug; and Henry, at the head of a troop of underpaid assistants, is hard at work clearing. The part clearing you will see from the map; from the house run down to the stream side, up the stream nearly as high as the garden; then back to the star which I have just added to the map.

My long, silent contests in the forest have had a strange effect on me. The unconcealed vitality of these vegetables, their exuberant number and strength, the attempts — I can use no other word — of lianas to enwrap and capture the intruder, the awful silence, the knowledge that all my efforts are only like the performance of an actor, the thing of a moment, and the wood will silently and swiftly heal them up with fresh effervescence; the cunning sense of the tuitui, suffering itself to be touched with wind-swayed grasses and not minding — but let the grass be moved by a man, and it shuts up; the whole silent battle, murder, and slow death of the contending forest; weigh upon the imagination. My poem the *Woodman* stands; but I have taken refuge in a new story, which just shot through me like a bullet in one

of my moments of awe, alone in that tragic
jungle : —

The High Woods of Ulufanua.[1]

1. A South Sea Bridal.
2. Under the Ban.
3. Savao and Faavao.
4. Cries in the High Wood.
5. Rumour full of Tongues.
6. The Hour of Peril.
7. The Day of Vengeance.

It is very strange, very extravagant, I
dare say; but it 's varied, and picturesque,
and has a pretty love affair, and ends well.
Ulufanua is a lovely Samoan word, ulu =
grove; fanua = land; grove-land — "the
tops of the high trees." Savao, "sacred to
the wood," and Faavao, "wood-ways," are
the names of two of the characters, Ulufanua
the name of the supposed island.

I am very tired, and rest off to-day from
all but letters. Fanny is quite done up;

---

[1] Afterwards changed into *The Beach of Falesá* (see
below, Letters VIII. X. XI.).

she could not sleep last night, something 1890
it seemed like asthma — I trust not. I Nov.
suppose Lloyd will be about, so you can
give him the benefit of this long scrawl.[1]
Never say that I *can't* write a letter, say
that I don't. — Yours ever, my dearest
fellow,   R. L. S.

Later on Friday.

The guid wife had bread to bake, and
she baked it in a pan, O! But between
whiles she was down with me weeding
sensitive in the paddock. The men have
but now passed over it; I was round in
that very place to see the weeding was
done thoroughly, and already the reptile
springs behind our heels. Tuitui is a
truly strange beast, and gives food for
thought. I am nearly sure — I cannot yet
be quite, I mean to experiment, when I am
less on the hot chase of the beast — that,
even at the instant he shrivels up his

[1] Mr. Lloyd Osbourne was at this time absent from his
family on a visit to England.

1890
Nov. leaves, he strikes his prickles downward
so as to catch the uprooting finger; instinc-
tive, say the gabies; but so is man's
impulse to strike out. One thing that
takes and holds me is to see the strange
variation in the propagation of alarm among
these rooted beasts; at times it spreads to
a radius (I speak by the guess of the eye)
of five or six inches; at times only one
individual plant appears frightened at a
time. We tried how long it took one to
recover; 't is a sanguine creature; it is all
abroad again before (I guess again) two
minutes. It is odd how difficult in this
world it is to be armed. The double
armour of this plant betrays it. In a thick
tuft, where the leaves disappear, I thrust
in my hand, and the bite of the thorns
betrays the topmost stem. In the open
again, and when I hesitate if it be clover,
a touch on the leaves, and its fine sense
and retractile action betrays its identity at
once. Yet it has one gift incomparable.
Rome had virtue and knowledge; Rome

perished. The sensitive plant has indigestible seeds — so they say — and it will
flourish for ever.   I give my advice thus to
a young plant — have a strong root, a weak
stem, and an indigestible seed; so you will
outlast the eternal city, and your progeny
will clothe mountains, and the irascible
planter will blaspheme in vain.   The weak
point of tuitui is that its stem is strong.

Supplementary Page.

Here beginneth the third lesson, which
is not from the planter but from a less
estimable character, the writer of books.

I want you to understand about this
South Sea book.[1]   The job is immense;
I stagger under material.   I have seen the
first big *tache*.   It was necessary to see the

[1] *The South Seas: a Record of Three Cruises:* such was
to be the title of the projected book, which was to narrate
the experiences of the author and his family on their recent
Pacific voyages, first in the yacht *Casco,* and afterwards in
the traders *Equator* and *Janet Nicoll.* His friends looked
forward to it with the hope that it would surpass his early
books of travels by all the difference between the beauty
and strangeness of the tropic islands and the homeliness
of the banks of Sambre and Oise or the desolation of the
Cevennes. But the material, perhaps from its too great

smaller ones; the letters were at my hand
for the purpose, but I was not going to
lose this experience; and instead of writing
mere letters, have poured out a lot of stuff
for the book. How this works and fits,
time is to show. But I believe, in time,
I shall get the whole thing in form. Now,
up to date, that is all my design, and I beg
to warn you till we have the whole (or
much) of the stuff together, you can hardly
judge — and I can hardly judge. Such a
mass of stuff is to be handled, if possible,
without repetition — so much foreign
matter to be introduced — if possible with
perspicuity — and as much as can be, a
spirit of narrative to be preserved. You
will find that come stronger as I proceed,
and get the explanations worked through.

richness and novelty, perhaps from the author's desire to
impart solid information instead of mere impressions,
proved intractable in his hands; and the work never got
beyond a number of chapters in the form of letters, written
with much less than his usual felicity, which were published
in full in the *New York Sun* and, in part only, in *Black
and White*. See below for further reference to the labour
which this undertaking cost him and to his disappointment
with the result.

Problems of style are (as yet) dirt under my 1890
Nov. feet; my problem is architectural, creative — to get this stuff jointed and moving. If I can do that, I will trouble you for style; anybody might write it, and it would be splendid; well-engineered, the masses right, the blooming thing travelling — twig?

This I wanted you to understand, for lots of the stuff sent home is, I imagine, rot — and slovenly rot — and some of it pompous rot; and I want you to understand it's a *lay-in*.

Soon, if the tide of poeshie continues, I'll send you a whole lot to damn. You never said thank-you for the handsome tribute addressed to you from Apemama; [1] such is the gratitude of the world to the God-sent poick. Well, well: — "Vex not thou the poick's mind, With thy coriaceous ingratitude, The P. will be to your faults more than a little blind, And yours is a far from handsome attitude." Having thus dropped into poetry in a spirit of friend-

---

[1] The lines beginning " I heard the pulse of the besieging sea," printed *Longman's Magazine*, January, 1895.

ship, I have the honour to subscribe myself, Sir,

      Your obedient humble servant,

          Silas Wegg.

I suppose by this you will have seen the
lad — and his feet will have been in the
Monument — and his eyes beheld the face
of George.[1] Well!

There is much eloquence in a well!

    I am, Sir

    Yours

    The Epigrammatist

ROBERT LOUIS STEVENSON

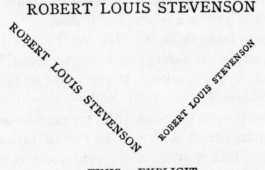

FINIS — EXPLICIT

[1] "The Monument" was his name for my house at the
British Museum, and George is my old faithful servant,
George Went; born 1819, died 1893.

II

Vailima, Tuesday, November 25th, 1890.

MY DEAR COLVIN, — I wanted to go out 1890
bright and early to go on with my survey. Nov.
You never heard of that. The world has
turned, and much water run under bridges,
since I stopped my diary. I have written
six more chapters of the book, all good I
potently believe, and given up, as a decep-
tion of the devil's, the High Woods. I
have been once down to Apia, to a huge
native feast at Seumanutafa's, the chief of
Apia. There was a vast mass of food,
crowds of people, the police charging
among them with whips, the whole in high
good humour on both sides; infinite noise;
and a historic event — Mr. Clarke, the
missionary, and his wife, assisted at a
native dance. On my return from this
function, I found work had stopped; no
more South Seas in my belly. Well,

1890
Nov.
Henry had cleared a great deal of our bush on a contract, and it ought to be measured. I set myself to the task with a tape-line; it seemed a dreary business; then I borrowed a prismatic compass, and tackled the task afresh. I have no books; I had not touched an instrument nor given a thought to the business since the year of grace 1871; you can imagine with what interest I sat down yesterday afternoon to reduce my observations; five triangles I had taken; all five came right, to my ineffable joy. Our dinner — the lowest we have ever been — consisted of *one avocado pear* between Fanny and me, a ship's biscuit for the guidman, white bread for the Missis, and red wine for the twa. No salt horse, even, in all Vailima! After dinner Henry came, and I began to teach him decimals; you would n't think I knew them myself after so long desuetude!

I could not but wonder how Henry stands his evenings here; the Polynesian loves gaiety — I feed him with decimals,

the mariner's compass, derivations, gram-
mar, and the like; delecting myself, after
the manner of my race, *moult tristement.*
I suck my paws; I live for my dexterities
and by my accomplishments; even my
clumsinesses are my joy — my woodcuts,
my stumbling on the pipe, this surveying
even — and even weeding sensitive; anything to do with the mind, with the eye,
with the hand — with a part of *me;* diver-
sion flows in these ways for the dreary
man. But gaiety is what these children
want; to sit in a crowd, tell stories and
pass jests, to hear one another laugh and
scamper with the girls. It's good fun,
too, I believe, but not for R. L. S., *ætat.*
40. Which I am now past forty, Custodian,
and not one penny the worse that I can
see; as amusable as ever; to be on board
ship is reward enough for me; give me the
wages of going on — in a schooner! Only,
if ever I were gay, which I misremember,
I am gay no more. And here is poor
Henry passing his evenings on my intel-

lectual husks, which the professors masticated; keeping the accounts of the estate — all wrong I have no doubt — I keep no check, beyond a very rough one; marching in with a cloudy brow, and the day-book under his arm; tackling decimals, coming with cases of conscience — how would an English chief behave in such a case? etc.; and, I am bound to say, on any glimmer of a jest, lapsing into native hilarity as a tree straightens itself after the wind is by. The other night I remembered my old friend — I believe yours also — Scholastikos, and administered the crow and the anchor — they were quite fresh to Samoan ears (this implies a very early severance) — and I thought the anchor would have made away with my Simelé altogether.

Fanny's time, in this interval, has been largely occupied in contending publicly with wild swine. We have a black sow; we call her Jack Sheppard; impossible to confine her — impossible also for her to be confined! To my sure knowledge she has

been in an interesting condition for longer
than any other sow in story; else she had
long died the death; as soon as she is
brought to bed, she shall count her days.
I suppose that sow has cost us in days'
labour from thirty to fifty dollars; as many
as eight boys (at a dollar a day) have been
twelve hours in chase of her. Now it is
supposed that Fanny has outwitted her;
she grins behind broad planks in what was
once the cook-house. She is a wild pig;
far handsomer than any tame; and when
she found the cook-house was too much for
her methods of evasion, she lay down on
the floor and refused food and drink for a
whole Sunday. On Monday morning, she
relapsed, and now eats and drinks like a
little man. I am reminded of an incident.
Two Sundays ago, the sad word was
brought that the sow was out again; this
time she had carried another in her flight.
Moors and I and Fanny were strolling up
to the garden, and there by the waterside
we saw the black sow, looking guilty. It

seemed to me beyond words; but Fanny's
cri du cœur was delicious: "G-r-r!" she
cried; "nobody loves you!"

I would I could tell you the moving
story of our cart and cart-horses; the latter
are dapple-grey, about sixteen hands, and
of enormous substance; the former was a
kind of red and green shandry-dan with
a driving bench; plainly unfit to carry
lumber or to face our road. (Remember
that the last third of my road, about a
mile, is all made out of a bridle-track by
my boys — and my dollars.) It was supposed a white man had been found — an
ex-German artilleryman — to drive this
last; he proved incapable and drunken;
the gallant Henry, who had never driven
before, and knew nothing about horses —
except the rats and weeds that flourish on
the islands — volunteered; Moors accepted,
proposing to follow and supervise: despatched his work and started after. No
cart! he hurried on up the road — no cart.
Transfer the scene to Vailima, where on a

sudden to Fanny and me, the cart appears, apparently at a hard gallop, some two hours before it was expected; Henry radiantly ruling chaos from the bench. It stopped: it was long before we had time to remark that the axle was twisted like the letter L. Our first care was the horses. There they stood, black with sweat, the sweat raining from them — literally raining — their heads down, their feet apart — and blood running thick from the nostrils of the mare. We got out Fanny's underclothes — could n't find anything else but our blankets — to rub them down, and in about half an hour we had the blessed satisfaction to see one after the other take a bite or two of grass. But it was a toucher; a little more and these steeds would have been foundered.

Monday, 31st? November.

Near a week elapsed, and no journal. On Monday afternoon, Moors rode up and I rode down with him, dined, and went

over in the evening to the American Consulate; present, Consul-General Sewall,
Lieut. Parker and Mrs. Parker, Lafarge
the American decorator, Adams an American historian; we talked late, and it was
arranged I was to write up for Fanny, and
we should both dine on the morrow.

On the Friday, I was all forenoon in the
Mission House, lunched at the German
Consulate, went on board the *Sperber*
(German war ship) in the afternoon, called
on my lawyer on my way out to American
Consulate, and talked till dinner time with
Adams, whom I am supplying with intro-
ductions and information for Tahiti and
the Marquesas. Fanny arrived a wreck,
and had to lie down. The moon rose, one
day past full, and we dined in the veranda,
a good dinner on the whole; talk with
Lafarge about art and the lovely dreams of
art students.[1] Remark by Adams, which

[1] Mr. John Lafarge of New York, one of the most
original and refined of living artists, whose record of his
holiday in the South Seas, in the shape of a series of

took me briskly home to the Monument 1890
Nov. — "I only liked one *young* woman — and that was Mrs. Procter." [1] Henry James would like that. Back by moonlight in the consulate boat — Fanny being too tired to walk — to Moors's. Saturday, I left Fanny to rest, and was off early to the Mission, where the politics are thrilling just now. The native pastors (to every one's surprise) have moved of themselves in the matter of the native dances, desiring the restrictions to be removed, or rather to be made dependent on the character of the dance. Clarke, who had feared censure and all kinds of trouble, is, of

---

water-color sketches of the scenery and people (with a catalogue full of interesting notes and observations) has been one of the features of the Champ de Mars Salon this year, and will, it may be hoped, be exhibited in London by the time these pages are published.

[1] Mrs. B. W. Procter, the step-daughter of Basil Montagu and widow of Barry Cornwall. The death of this spirited veteran in 1888 snapped away one of the last links with the days and memories of Keats and Coleridge. A shrewd and not too indulgent judge of character, she took R. L. S. into warm favour at first sight, and never spoke of or inquired after him but with unwonted tenderness.

course, rejoicing greatly.   A characteristic
feature: the argument of the pastors was
handed in in the form of a fictitious narrative of the voyage of one Mr. Pye, an English traveller, and his conversation with a
chief; there are touches of satire in this
educational romance.   Mr. Pye, for instance, admits that he knows nothing about
the Bible.   At the Mission I was sought
out by Henry in a devil of an agitation;
he has been made the victim of a forgery
—a crime hitherto unknown in Samoa.   I
had to go to Folau, the chief judge here,
in the matter.   Folau had never heard of
the offence, and begged to know what was
the punishment; there may be lively times
in forgery ahead.   It seems the sort of
crime to tickle a Polynesian.   After lunch
—you can see what a busy three days I am
describing — we set off to ride home.   My
Jack was full of the devil of corn and too
much grass, and no work.   I had to ride
ahead and leave Fanny behind.   He is a
most gallant little rascal is my Jack, and

takes the whole way as hard as the rider
pleases. Single incident: half-way up, I
find my boys upon the road and stop and
talk with Henry in his character of ganger,
as long as Jack will suffer me. Fanny
drones in after; we make a show of eating
— or I do — she goes to bed about half-past
six! I write some verses, read Irving's
Washington, and follow about half-past
eight. O, one thing more I did, in a pro-
phetic spirit. I had made sure Fanny was
not fit to be left alone, and wrote before
turning in a letter to Chalmers, telling him
I could not meet him in Auckland at this
time. By eleven at night, Fanny got me
wakened — she had tried twice in vain —
and I found her very bad. Thence till
three, we laboured with mustard poultices,
laudanum, soda and ginger — Heavens!
was n't it cold; the land breeze was as cold
as a river; the moon was glorious in the paddock, and the great boughs and the black
shadows of our trees were inconceivable.
But it was a poor time.

Sunday morning found Fanny, of course,
a complete wreck, and myself not very
brilliant. Paul had to go to Vailele *re*
cocoa-nuts; it was doubtful if he could be
back by dinner; never mind, said I, I'll
take dinner when you return. Off set
Paul. I did an hour's work, and then
tackled the house work. I did it beautiful:
the house was a picture, it resplended of
propriety. Presently Mr. Moors's Andrew
rode up; I heard the doctor was at the
Forest House and sent a note to him; and
when he came, I heard my wife telling him
she had been in bed all day, and that was
why the house was so dirty! Was it grate-
ful? Was it politic? Was it TRUE? —
Enough! In the interval, up marched
little L. S., one of my neighbours, all in
his Sunday white linens; made a fine
salute, and demanded the key of the kitchen
in German and English. And he cooked
dinner for us, like a little man, and had it
on the table and the coffee ready by the
hour. Paul had arranged me this surprise.

Some time later, Paul returned himself with a fresh surprise on hand; he was almost sober; nothing but a hazy eye distinguished him from Paul of the week days: *vivat!*

On the evening I cannot dwell. All the horses got out of the paddock, went across, and smashed my neighbour's garden into a big hole. How little the amateur conceives a farmer's troubles. I went out at once with a lantern, staked up a gap in the hedge, was kicked at by a chestnut mare, who straightway took to the bush; and came back. A little after, they had found another gap, and the crowd were all abroad again. What has happened to our own garden nobody yet knows.

Fanny had a fair night, and we are both tolerable this morning, only the yoke of correspondence lies on me heavy. I beg you will let this go on to my mother. I got such a good start in your letter, that I kept on at it, and I have neither time nor energy for more.

Yours ever,

R. L. S.

Something new.

1890
Nov.
I was called from my letters by the voice of Mr. ———, who had just come up with a load of wood, roaring, "Henry! Henry! Bring six boys!" I saw there was something wrong, and ran out. The cart, half unloaded, had upset with the mare in the shafts; she was all cramped together and all tangled up in harness and cargo, the off shaft pushing her over, Mr. ——— holding her up by main strength, and right alongside of her — where she must fall if she went down — a deadly stick of a tree like a lance. I could not but admire the wisdom and faith of this great brute; I never saw the riding-horse that would not have lost its life in such a situation; but the cart-elephant patiently waited and was saved. It was a stirring three minutes, I can tell you.

I forgot in talking of Saturday to tell of one incident which will particularly interest my mother. I met Dr. D. from Savaii, and had an age-long talk about

Edinburgh folk; it was very pleasant. He
has been studying in Edinburgh, along with his son; a pretty relation. He told me he knew nobody but college people: "I was altogether a student," he said with glee. He seems full of cheerfulness and thick-set energy. I feel as if I could put him in a novel with effect; and ten to one, if I know more of him, the image will be only blurred.

Tuesday, Dec. 2nd.

I should have told you yesterday that all my boys were got up for their work in moustaches and side-whiskers of some sort of blacking — I suppose wood-ash. It was a sight of joy to see them return at night, axe on shoulder, feigning to march like soldiers, a choragus with a loud voice singing out, "March — step! March — step!" in imperfect recollection of some drill.

Fanny seems much revived.

R. L. S.

III

MY DEAR COLVIN, — I do not say my Jack is anything extraordinary; he is only an island horse; and the profane might call him a Punch; and his face is like a donkey's; and natives have ridden him, and he has no mouth in consequence, and occasionally shies. But his merits are equally surprising; and I don't think I should ever have known Jack's merits if I had not been riding up of late on moonless nights. Jack is a bit of a dandy; he loves to misbehave in a gallant manner, above all on Apia Street, and when I stop to speak to people, they say (Dr. Stuebel the German consul said about three days ago), "Oh, what a wild horse! it cannot be safe to ride him." Such a remark is Jack's reward, and represents his ideal of fame. Now when I start out of Apia on a dark night, you should see my changed horse; at a fast steady walk, with his head down, and sometimes his nose to the ground — when he wants to do that he asks for his head with a little eloquent polite movement indescribable — he climbs the long ascent and threads the darkest of the wood. The first night I came it was starry; and it was singular to see the starlight drip down into the crypt of the wood, and shine in the open end of the road, as bright as moonlight at home; but the crypt itself was proof, blackness lived in it. The next night it was raining. We left the lights of Apia and passed into limbo. Jack finds a way for himself, but he does not calculate for my height above the saddle; and I am directed forward, all braced up for a crouch and holding my switch upright in front of me. It is curiously interesting. In the forest, the dead wood is phosphorescent; some nights the whole ground is strewn with it, so that it seems like a

grating over a pale hell; doubtless this is
one of the things that feed the night fears
of the natives; and I am free to confess
that in a night of trackless darkness where
all else is void, these pallid *ignes suppositi*
have a fantastic appearance, rather bogey
even.   One night, when it was very dark,
a man had put out a little lantern by the
wayside to show the entrance to his ground.
I saw the light, as I thought, far ahead,
and supposed it was a pedestrian coming to
meet me; I was quite taken by surprise
when it struck in my face and passed
behind me.   Jack saw it, and he was ap-
palled; do you think he thought of shy-
ing?   No, sir, not in the dark; in the
dark Jack knows he is on duty; and he
went past that lantern steady and swift;
only, as he went, he groaned and shud-
dered.   For about 2500 of Jack's steps we
only pass one house — that where the
lantern was; and about 1500 of these are
in the darkness of the pit.   But now the
moon is on tap again, and the roads lighted.

I have been exploring up the Vaituliga; 1890 Dec. see your map. It comes down a wonderful fine glen; at least 200 feet of cliffs on

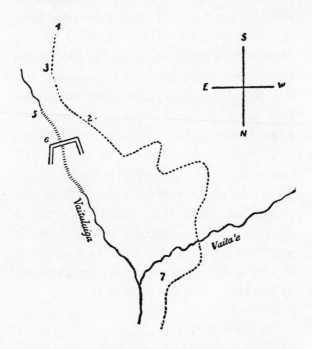

either hand, winding like a corkscrew, great forest trees filling it. At the top

there ought to be a fine double fall; but
the stream evades it by a fault and passes
underground.   Above the fall it runs (at
this season) full and very gaily in a shallow
valley, some hundred yards before the head
of the glen.   Its course is seen full of
grasses, like a flooded meadow; that is the
sink! beyond the grave of the grasses, the
bed lies dry.   Near this upper part there
is a great show of ruinous pig-walls; a
village must have stood near by.

To walk from our house to Wreck Hill
(when the path is buried in fallen trees)
takes one about half an hour, I think; to
return not more than twenty minutes; I
dare say fifteen.   Hence I should guess it
was three-quarters of a mile.   I had meant
to join on my explorations passing eastward
by the sink; but, Lord! how it rains.

(*Later.*)

I went out this morning with a pocket
compass and walked in a varying direction,
perhaps on an average S. by W., 1754
paces.   Then I struck into the bush, N.

W. by N., hoping to strike the Vaituliga above the falls. Now I have it plotted out I see I should have gone W. or even W by S.; but it is not easy to guess. For 600 weary paces I struggled through the bush, and then came on the stream below the gorge, where it was comparatively easy to get down to it. In the place where I struck it, it made cascades about a little isle, and was running about N.E., 20 to 30 feet wide, as deep as to my knee, and piercing cold. I tried to follow it down, and keep the run of its direction and my paces; but when I was wading to the knees and the waist in mud, poison brush, and rotted wood, bound hand and foot in lianas, shovelled unceremoniously off the one shore and driven to try my luck upon the other — I saw I should have hard enough work to get my body down, if my mind rested. It was a damnable walk; certainly not half a mile as the crow flies, but a real bucketer for hardship. Once I had to pass the stream where it flowed between banks about three feet high. To get the easier down, I swung myself by a wild-cocoanut — (so called, it bears bunches of scarlet nutlets) — which grew upon the brink. As I so swung, I received a crack on the head that knocked me all abroad. Impossible to guess what tree had taken a shy at me. So many towered above, one over the other, and the missile, whatever it was, dropped in the stream and was gone before I had recovered my wits. (I scarce know what I write, so hideous a Niagara of rain roars, shouts, and demonizes on the iron roof — it is pitch dark too — the lamp lit at 5!) It was a blessed thing when I struck my own road; and I got home, neat for lunch time, one of the most wonderful mud statues ever witnessed. In the afternoon I tried again, going up the other path by the garden, but was early drowned out; came home, plotted out what I had done, and then wrote this truck to you.

Fanny has been quite ill with ear-ache.

She won't go,[1] hating the sea at this wild season; I don't like to leave her; so it drones on, steamer after steamer, and I guess it 'll end by no one going at all. She is in a dreadful misfortune at this hour; a case of kerosene having burst in the kitchen. A little while ago it was the carpenter's horse that trod in a nest of fourteen eggs, and made an omelette of our hopes. The farmer's lot is not a happy one. And it looks like some real uncompromising bad weather too. I wish Fanny's ear were well. Think of parties in Monuments! think of me in Skerryvore, and now of this. It don't look like a part of the same universe to me. Work is quite laid aside; I have worked myself right out.

Christmas Eve.

Yesterday, who could write? My wife near crazy with ear-ache; the rain descending in white crystal rods and playing hell's tattoo, like a *tutti* of battering rams, on

[1] On a projected expedition to Sydney.

our sheet-iron roof; the wind passing high
overhead with a strange dumb mutter, or
striking us full, so that all the huge trees
in the paddock cried aloud, and wrung
their hands, and brandished their vast
arms. The horses stood in the shed like
things stupid. The sea and the flagship
lying on the jaws of the bay vanished in
sheer rain. All day it lasted; I locked up
my papers in the iron box, in case it was a
hurricane, and the house might go. We
went to bed with mighty uncertain feelings; far more than on shipboard, where
you have only drowning ahead — whereas
here you have a smash of beams, a shower
of sheet-iron, and a blind race in the dark
and through a whirlwind for the shelter of
an unfinished stable — and my wife with
ear-ache! Well, well, this morning, we
had word from Apia; a hurricane was
looked for, the ships were to leave the bay
by 10 A. M.; it is now 3.30, and the flagship is still a fixture, and the wind round
in the blessed east, so I suppose the danger

is over. But heaven is still laden; the 1890
Dec. day dim, with frequent rattling bucketfuls of rain; and just this moment (as I write) a squall went overhead, scarce striking us, with that singular, solemn noise of its passage, which is to me dreadful. I have always feared the sound of wind beyond everything. In my hell it would always blow a gale.

I have been all day correcting proofs, and making out a new plan for our house. The other was too dear to be built now, and it was a hard task to make a smaller house that would suffice for the present, and not be a mere waste of money in the future. I believe I have succeeded; I have taken care of my study anyway.

Two favours I want to ask of you. First, I wish you to get "Pioneering in New Guinea," by J. Chalmers. It's a missionary book, and has less pretensions to be literature than Spurgeon's sermons. Yet I think even through that, you will see some of the traits of the hero that wrote it; a man that took me fairly by storm for the most attractive, simple, brave, and interesting man in the whole Pacific. He is away now to go up the Fly River; a desperate venture, it is thought; he is quite a Livingstone card.

Second, try and keep yourself free next winter; and if my means can be stretched so far, I 'll come to Egypt and we 'll meet at Shepheard's Hotel, and you 'll put me in my place, which I stand in need of badly by this time.   Lord, what bully times! I suppose I 'll come per British Asia, or whatever you call it, and avoid all cold, and might be in Egypt about November as ever was — eleven months from now or rather less.   But do not let us count our chickens.

Last night three piglings were stolen from one of our pig-pens. The great Lafaele appeared to my wife uneasy, so she engaged him in conversation on the subject, and played upon him the following engaging trick. You advance your two forefingers towards the sitter's eyes; he closes them, whereupon you substitute (on his eyelids) the fore and middle fingers of the left hand; and with your right (which he supposes engaged) you tap him on the head and back. When you let him open his eyes, he sees you withdrawing the two forefingers. "What that?" asked Lafaele. "My devil," says Fanny. "I wake um, my devil. All right now. He go catch the man that catch my pig." About an hour afterwards, Lafaele came for further particulars. "Oh, all right," my wife says. "By and by, that man he sleep, devil go sleep same place. By and by, that man plenty sick. I no care. What for he take my pig?" Lafaele cares plenty; I don't think he is the man, though he may be; but he knows him, and most likely will eat some of that pig to-night. He will not eat with relish.

Saturday, 27th.

It cleared up suddenly after dinner, and
my wife and I saddled up and off to Apia,
whence we did not return till yesterday
morning. Christmas Day I wish you could
have seen our party at table. H. J. Moors
at one end with my wife, I at the other
with Mrs. M. between us two native
women, Carruthers the lawyer, Moors's
two shop-boys — Walters and A. M. the
quadroon — and the guests of the evening,
Shirley Baker, the defamed and much-
accused man of Tonga, and his son, with
the artificial joint to his arm — where the
assassins shot him in shooting at his
father. Baker's appearance is not unlike
John Bull on a cartoon; he is highly
interesting to speak to, as I had expected;
I found he and I had many common interests, and were engaged in puzzling over
many of the same difficulties. After dinner
it was quite pretty to see our Christmas
party, it was so easily pleased and prettily
behaved. In the morning I should say I

had been to lunch at the German consulate, where I had as usual a very pleasant time. I shall miss Dr. Stuebel[1] much when he leaves, and when Adams and Lafarge go also, it will be a great blow. I am getting spoiled with all this good society.

On Friday morning, I had to be at my house affairs before seven; and they kept me in Apia till past ten, disputing, and consulting about brick and stone and native and hydraulic lime, and cement and sand, and all sorts of otiose details about the chimney — just what I fled from in my father's office twenty years ago; I should have made a languid engineer. Rode up with the carpenter. Ah, my wicked Jack! on Christmas Eve, as I was taking the saddle bag off, he kicked at me, and fetched me too, right on the shin. On Friday, being annoyed at the carpenter's horse having a longer trot, he uttered a shrill

---

[1] See *A Footnote to History* for more in praise of Dr. Stuebel, and of his exceptional deserts among white officials in Samoa.

cry and tried to bite him! Alas, alas, these are like old days; my dear Jack is a Bogue,[1] but I cannot strangle Jack into submission.

I have given up the big house for just now; we go ahead right away with a small one, which should be ready in two months, and I suppose will suffice for just now.

O I know I have n't told you about our *aitu*, have I? It is a lady, *Aitu fafine:* she lives on the mountain-side; her presence is heralded by the sound of a gust of wind; a sound very common in the high woods; when she catches you, I do not know what happens; but in practice she is avoided, so I suppose she does more than pass the time of day. The great *aitu Saumai-afe* was once a living woman; and became an *aitu*, no one understands how; she lives in a stream at the well-head, her hair is red, she appears as a lovely young lady, her bust particularly admired, to

---

[1] The wicked Skye-terrier of Bournemouth days, celebrated in the essay *On the Character of Dogs.*

handsome young men; these die, her love being fatal; — as a handsome youth she has been known to court damsels with the like result, but this is very rare; as an old crone she goes about and asks for water, and woe to them who are uncivil! *Saumai-afe* means literally, " Come here a thous- and!" A good name for a lady of her manners. My *aitu fafine* does not seem to be in the same line of business. It is unsafe to be a handsome youth in Samoa; a young man died from her favours last month — so we said on this side of the island; on the other, where he died, it was not so certain. I, for one, blame it on Madam *Saumai-afe* without hesitation.

Example of the farmer's sorrows. I slipped out on the balcony a moment ago. It is a lovely morning, cloudless, smoking hot, the breeze not yet arisen. Looking west, in front of our new house, I saw two heads of Indian corn wagging, and the rest and all nature stock still. As I looked, one of the stalks subsided and disappeared.

1890
Dec. I dashed out to the rescue; two small pigs
were deep in the grass — quite hid till
within a few yards — gently but swiftly
demolishing my harvest. Never be a
farmer.

12.30 p. m.

I while away the moments of digestion
by drawing you a faithful picture of my
morning. When I had done writing as
above it was time to clean our house.
When I am working, it falls on my wife
alone, but to-day we had it between us;
she did the bedroom, I the sitting-room,
in fifty-seven minutes of really most un-
palatable labour. Then I changed every
stitch, for I was wet through, and sat down
and played on my pipe till dinner was
ready, mighty pleased to be in a mildly
habitable spot once more. The house had
been neglected for near a week, and was a
hideous spot; my wife's ear and our visit
to Apia being the causes: our Paul we
prefer not to see upon that theatre, and
God knows he has plenty to do elsewhere.

I am glad to look out of my back door
and see the boys smoothing the foundations of the new house; this is all very jolly, but six months of it has satisfied me; we have too many things for such close quarters; to work in the midst of all the myriad misfortunes of the planter's life, seated in a Dyonisius' (can't spell him) ear, whence I catch every complaint, mishap and contention, is besides the devil; and the hope of a cave of my own inspires me with lust. O to be able to shut my own door and make my own confusion! O to have the brown paper and the matches and "make a hell of my own " once more!

I do not bother you with all my troubles in these outpourings; the troubles of the farmer are inspiriting — they are like difficulties out hunting — a fellow rages at the time and rejoices to recall and to commemorate them. My troubles have been financial. It is hard to arrange wisely interests so distributed. America, England, Samoa, Sydney, everywhere I have an end of liability hanging out and some shelf of credit hard by; and to juggle all these and build a dwelling-place here, and check expense — a thing I am ill fitted for — you can conceive what a night-mare it is at times. Then God knows I have not been idle. But since *The Master*[1] nothing has come to raise any coins. I believe the springs are dry at home, and now I am worked out, and can no more at all. A holiday is required.

Dec. 28th. I have got unexpectedly to work again, and feel quite dandy. Good-bye.

R. L. S.

[1] *Of Ballantrae.*

IV

S. Lübeck, between Apia and Sydney.
Jan. 17th, 1891.

MY DEAR COLVIN, — The Faamasino
Sili, or Chief Justice, to speak your low
language, has arrived. I had ridden down
with Henry and Lafaele; the sun was
down, the night was close at hand, so we
rode fast; just as I came to the corner of
the road before Apia, I heard a gun fire;
and lo, there was a great crowd at the end
of the pier, and the troops out, and a chief
or two in the height of Samoa finery, and
Seumanu coming in his boat (the oarsmen
all in uniform), bringing the Faamasino
Sili sure enough. It was lucky he was no
longer; the natives would not have waited
many weeks. But think of it, as I sat in
the saddle at the outside of the crowd
(looking, the English consul said, as if I
were commanding the manœuvres), I was

nearly knocked down by a stampede of the
three consuls; they had been waiting their
guest at the Matafele end, and some
wretched intrigue among the whites had
brought him to Apia, and the consuls had
to run all the length of the town and come
too late.

The next day was a long one; I was at a
marriage of G. the banker to Fanua, the
virgin of Apia. Bride and bridesmaids
were all in the old high dress; the ladies
were all native; the men, with the exception of Seumanu, all white.

It was quite a pleasant party, and while
we were waiting, we had a bird's-eye view
of the public reception of the Chief Justice.
The best part of it were some natives in
war array; with blacked faces, turbans,
tapa kilts, and guns, they looked very
manly and purposelike. No, the best part
was poor old drunken Joe, the Portuguese
boatman, who seemed to think himself
specially charged with the reception, and
ended by falling on his knees before the

1891
Jan.

Chief Justice on the end of the pier and in full view of the whole town and bay. The natives pelted him with rotten bananas; how the Chief Justice took it I was too far off to see; but it was highly absurd.

I have commemorated my genial hopes for the regimen of the Faamasino Sili in the following canine verses, which, if you at all guess how to read them, are very pretty in movement, and (unless he be a mighty good man) too true in sense.

We're quarrelling, the villages, we've beaten the wooden
    drums,
Sa femisai o nu'u, sa taia o pate,
Is expounded there by the justice,
Ua Atuatuvale a le faamasino e,
The chief justice, the terrified justice,
Le faamasino sili, le faamasino se,
Is on the point of running away the justice,
O le a solasola le faamasino e,
The justice denied any influence, the terrified justice,
O le faamasino le ai a, le faamasino se,
O le a solasola le faamasino e.

Well, after this excursion into tongues that have never been alive — though I assure you we have one capital book in the

language, a book of fables by an old missionary of the unpromising name of Pratt,
which is simply the best and the most
literary version of the fables known to me.
I suppose I should except La Fontaine,
but L. F. takes a long time; these are
brief as the books of our childhood, and
full of wit and literary colour; and O,
Colvin, what a tongue it would be to write,
if one only knew it — and there were only
readers. Its curse in common use is an
incredible left-handed wordiness; but in
the hands of a man like Pratt it is succinct
as Latin, compact of long rolling polysyl-
lables and little and often pithy particles,
and for beauty of sound a dream. Listen,
I quote from Pratt — this is good Samoan,
not canine —

1   2   3   4   1
O le afa,   ua taalili ai   le ulu vao,   ua pa mai   le faititili.

1 almost *wa*, 2 the two *a's* just distinguished, 3 the *ai* is practically suffixed to
the verb, 4 almost *vow*. The excursion
has prolonged itself.

I started by the *Lübeck* to meet Lloyd
and my mother; there were many reasons
for and against; the main reason against
was the leaving of Fanny alone in her
blessed cabin, which has been somewhat
remedied by my carter, Mr. ——, putting
up in the stable and messing with her; but
perhaps desire of change decided me not
well, though I do think I ought to see an
occulist, being very blind indeed, and
sometimes unable to read. Anyway I left,
the only cabin passenger, four and a kid in
the second cabin, and a dear voyage it had
like to have proved. Close to Fiji (choose
a worse place on the map) we broke our
shaft early one morning; and when or
where we might expect to fetch land or
meet with any ship, I would like you to
tell me. The Pacific is absolutely desert.
I have sailed there now some years; and
scarce ever seen a ship except in port or
close by; I think twice. It was the hurricane season besides and hurricane waters.
Well, our chief engineer got the shaft — it

was the middle crank shaft — mended;
thrice it was mended, and twice broke
down; but now keeps up — only we dare
not stop, for it is almost impossible to
start again. The captain in the meanwhile
crowded her with sail; fifteen sails in all,
every stay being gratified with a stay-sail,
a boat-boom sent aloft for a maintop-
gallant yard, and the derrick of a crane
brought in service as bowsprit. All the
time we have had a fine, fair wind and a
smooth sea; to-day at noon our run was
203 miles (if you please!), and we are
within some 360 miles of Sydney. Probably there has never been a more gallant
success; and I can say honestly it was well
worked for. No flurry, no high words, no
long faces; only hard work and honest
thought; a pleasant, manly business to be
present at. All the chances were we
might have been six weeks — ay, or three
months at sea — or never turned up at all,
and now it looks as though we should reach
our destination some five days too late.

V

[*On Board Ship between Sydney and Apia,*
Feb. 1891.]

MY DEAR COLVIN, — The *Janet Nicoll* 1891
Feb.
stuff was rather worse than I had looked
for; you have picked out all that is fit to
stand, bar two others (which I don't dislike) — the Port of Entry and the House
of Temoana; that is for a present opinion;
I may condemn these also ere I have done.
By this time you should have another
Marquesan letter, the worst of the lot, I
think; and seven Paumotu letters, which
are not far out of the vein, as I wish it; I
am in hopes the Hawaiian stuff is better
yet: time will show, and time will make
perfect. Is something of this sort prac-
ticable for the dedication?

TERRA MARIQUE

PER PERICULA PER ARDUA

AMICAE COMITI

D. D.

AMANS VIATOR

'T is a first shot concocted this morning in my berth: I had always before been trying it in English, which insisted on being either insignificant or fulsome: I cannot think of a better word than *comes*, there being not the shadow of a Latin book on board; yet sure there is some other. Then *viator* (though it *sounds* all right) is doubtful; it has too much, perhaps, the sense of wayfarer? Last, will it mark sufficiently that I mean my wife? And first, how about blunders? I scarce wish it longer.

Have had a swingeing sharp attack in Sydney; beating the fields for two nights, Saturday and Sunday. Wednesday was brought on board, *tel quel*, a wonderful wreck; and now, Wednesday week, am a good deal picked up, but yet not quite a Samson, being still groggy afoot and vague in the head. My chess, for instance, which is usually a pretty strong game, and defies all rivalry aboard, is vacillating, devoid of resource and observation, and hitherto not covered with customary laurels. As for work, it is impossible. We shall be in the saddle before long, no doubt, and the pen once more couched. You must not expect a letter under these circumstances, but be very thankful for a note. Once at Samoa, I shall try to resume my late excellent habits, and delight you with journals, you unaccustomed, I unaccustomed; but it is never too late to mend.

It is vastly annoying that I cannot go even to Sydney without an attack; and heaven knows my life was anodyne. I only once dined with anybody; at the club with Wise; worked all morning — a terrible dead pull; a month only produced the imperfect embryos of two chapters; lunched in the boarding-house, played on my pipe; went out and did some of my messages; dined at a French restaurant, and returned to play draughts, whist, or Van John with my family. This makes a cheery life after Samoa; but it is n't what you call burning the candle at both ends, is it? (It appears

1891
Feb. to me not one word of this letter will be
legible by the time I am done with it, this
dreadful ink rubs off.) I have a strange
kind of novel under construction; it begins
about 1660 and ends 1830, or perhaps I
may continue it to 1875 or so, with another
life. One, two, three, four, five, six gen-
erations, perhaps seven, figure therein;
two of my old stories, "Delafield" and
"Shovel," are incorporated; it is to be told
in the third person, with some of the
brevity of history, some of the detail of
romance. *The Shovels of Newton French*
will be the name. The idea is an old one;
it was brought to birth by an accident; a
friend in the islands who picked up F.
Jenkin,[1] read a part, and said: "Do you
know, that's a strange book? I like it;

[1] Memoir of Fleeming Jenkin, by R. L. S. Prefixed to
*Papers Literary, Scientific, etc., by the late Fleeming Jenkin,
F.R.S., LL.D.*; 2 vols. London, Longmans, 1887. The
first chapters of this memoir consist of a genealogical
history of the family. Of "Delafield" I never heard;
the plan of "Shovel," which was to be in great part a
story of the Peninsula War, had been sketched out as
long ago as the seventies.

I don't believe the public will; but I like 1891
Feb. it." He thought it was a novel! "Very well," said I, "we 'll see whether the public will like it or not; they shall have the chance."

Yours ever,
R. L. S.

VI

1891
Mar.
MY DEAR S. C., — You probably expect that now I am back at Vailima I shall resume the practice of the diary letter. A good deal is changed. We are more; solitude does not attend me as before; the night is passed playing Van John for shells; and, what is not less important, I have just recovered from a severe illness, and am easily tired.

I will give you to-day. I sleep now in one of the lower rooms of the new house, where my wife has recently joined me. We have two beds, an empty case for a table, a chair, a tin basin, a bucket and a jug; next door in the dining-room, the carpenters camp on the floor, which is covered with their mosquito nets. Before the sun rises, at 5.45 or 5.50, Paul brings me tea, bread, and a couple of eggs; and

by about six I am at work.   I work in bed 1891
Mar.
— my bed is of mats, no mattress, sheets,
or filth — mats, a pillow, and a blanket —
and put in some three hours.   It was 9.5
this morning when I set off to the stream-
side to my weeding; where I toiled, man-
uring the ground with the best enricher,
human sweat, till the conch-shell was
blown from our verandah at 10.30.   At
eleven we dine; about half-past twelve I
tried (by exception) to work again, could
make nothing on't, and by one was on my
way to the weeding, where I wrought till
three.   Half-past five is our next meal,
and I read Flaubert's Letters till the hour
came round; dined, and then, Fanny having a cold, and I being tired, came over to
my den in the unfinished house, where I
now write to you, to the tune of the
carpenters' voices, and by the light — I
crave your pardon — by the twilight of
three vile candles filtered through the
medium of my mosquito bar.   Bad ink
being of the party, I write quite blindfold,

and can only hope you may be granted to
read that which I am unable to see while
writing.

I said I was tired; it is a mild phrase;
my back aches like toothache; when I shut
my eyes to sleep, I know I shall see before
them — a phenomenon to which both Fanny
and I are quite accustomed — endless vivid
deeps of grass and weed, each plant particular and distinct, so that I shall lie
inert in body, and transact for hours the
mental part of my day business, choosing
the noxious from the useful. And in my
dreams I shall be hauling on recalcitrants,
and suffering stings from nettles, stabs
from citron thorns, fiery bites from ants,
sickening resistances of mud and slime,
evasions of slimy roots, dead weight of
heat, sudden puffs of air, sudden starts
from bird-calls in the contiguous forest —
some mimicking my name, some laughter,
some the signal of a whistle, and living
over again at large the business of my
day.

1891
Mar.

Though I write so little, I pass all my hours of field-work in continual converse and imaginary correspondence. I scarce pull up a weed, but I invent a sentence on the matter to yourself; it does not get written; *autant en emportent les vents;* but the intent is there, and for me (in some sort) the companionship. To-day, for instance, we had a great talk. I was toiling, the sweat dripping from my nose, in the hot fit after a squall of rain: methought you asked me — frankly, was I happy. Happy (said I); I was only happy once; that was at Hyères; it came to an end from a variety of reasons, decline of health, change of place, increase of money, age with his stealing steps; since then, as before then, I know not what it means. But I know pleasure still; pleasure with a thousand faces, and none perfect, a thousand tongues all broken, a thousand hands, and all of them with scratching nails. High among these I place this delight of weeding out here alone by the garrulous

water, under the silence of the high wood,
broken by incongruous sounds of birds.
And take my life all through, look at it
fore and back, and upside down, — though
I would very fain change myself — I would
not change my circumstances, unless it
were to bring you here. And yet God
knows perhaps this intercourse of writing
serves as well; and I wonder, were you
here indeed, would I commune so continually with the thought of you. I say I
wonder for a form; I know, and I know I
should not.

So far and much further, the conversation went, while I groped in slime after
viscous roots, nursing and sparing little
spears of grass, and retreating (even with
outcry) from the prod of the wild lime. I
wonder if any one had ever the same attitude to Nature as I hold, and have held
for so long? This business fascinates me
like a tune or a passion; yet all the while
I thrill with a strong distaste. The horror
of the thing, objective and subjective, is

always present to my mind; the horror of creeping things, a superstitious horror of the void and the powers about me, the horror of my own devastation and continual murders. The life of the plants comes through my finger-tips, their struggles go to my heart like supplications. I feel myself blood-boltered; then I look back on my cleared grass, and count myself an ally in a fair quarrel, and make stout my heart.

It is but a little while since I lay sick in Sydney, beating the fields about the navy and Dean Swift and Dryden's Latin hymns; judge if I love this reinvigorating climate, where I can already toil till my head swims and every string in the poor jumping Jack (as he now lies in bed) aches with a kind of yearning strain, difficult to suffer in quiescence.

As for my damned literature,[1] God knows what a business it is, grinding along without a scrap of inspiration or a note of style. But it has to be ground, and

[1] *The South Sea Letters.*

the mill grinds exceeding slowly though not
particularly small. The last two chapters
have taken me considerably over a month,
and they are still beneath pity. This I
cannot continue, time not sufficing; and
the next will just have to be worse. All
the good I can express is just this; some
day, when style revisits me, they will be
excellent matter to rewrite. Of course,
my old cure of a change of work would
probably answer, but I cannot take it now.
The treadmill turns; and with a kind of
desperate cheerfulness, I mount the idle
stair. I have n't the least anxiety about
the book; unless I die, I shall find the
time to make it good; but the Lord
deliver me from the thought of the Letters!
However, the Lord has other things on
hand; and about six to-morrow, I shall
resume the consideration practically, and
face (as best I may) the fact of my incom-
petence and disaffection to the task. Toil
I do not spare; but fortune refuses me
success. We can do more, Whatever-his-

1891
Mar.

name-was, we can deserve it. But my misdesert began long since, by the acceptation of a bargain quite unsuitable to all my methods.[1]

To-day I have had a queer experience. My carter has from the first been using my horses for his own ends; when I left for Sydney, I put him on his honour to cease, and my back was scarce turned ere he was forfeit. I have only been waiting to discharge him; and to-day an occasion arose. I am so much *the old man virulent,* so readily stumble into anger, that I gave a deal of consideration to my bearing, and decided at last to imitate that of the late ——. Whatever he might have to say, this eminently effective controversialist maintained a frozen demeanour and a jeering smile. The frozen demeanour is beyond my reach; but I could try the jeering smile; did so, perceived its efficacy,

---

[1] The price advanced for these Letters was among the considerations which originally induced the writer to set out on his Pacific voyage.

kept in consequence my temper, and got
rid of my friend, myself composed and
smiling still, he white and shaking like an
aspen. He could explain everything; I
said it did not interest me. He said he
had enemies; I said nothing was more
likely. He said he was calumniated; with
all my heart, said I, but there are so many
liars, that I find it safer to believe them.
He said, in justice to himself, he must
explain: God forbid, I should interfere
with you, said I, with the same factitious
grin, but it can change nothing. So I
kept my temper, rid myself of an unfaith-
ful servant, found a method of conducting
similar interviews in the future, and fell
in my own liking. One thing more: I
learned a fresh tolerance for the dead ——;
he too had learned — perhaps had invented
— the trick of this manner; God knows what
weakness, what instability of feeling, lay
beneath. *Ce que c'est que de nous;* poor
human nature; that at past forty I must
adjust this hateful mask for the first time,

and rejoice to find it effective; that the effort of maintaining an external smile should confuse and embitter a man's soul.

To-day I have not weeded; I have written instead from six till eleven, from twelve till two; with the interruption of the inter-view aforesaid; a damned letter is written for the third time; I dread to read it, for I dare not give it a fourth chance — unless it be very bad indeed. Now I write you from my mosquito curtain, to the song of saws and planes and hammers, and wood clumping on the floor above; in a day of heavenly brightness; a bird twittering near by; my eye, through the open door, com-manding green meads, two or three forest trees casting their boughs against the sky, a forest-clad mountain-side beyond, and close in by the door-jamb a nick of the blue Pacific. It is March in England, bleak March, and I lie here with the great sliding doors wide open in an undershirt and p'jama trousers, and melt in the closure of mosquito bars, and burn to be out in the

1891
Mar. breeze. A few torn clouds — not white,
the sun has tinged them a warm pink —
swim in heaven. In which blessed and
fair day, I have to make faces and speak
bitter words to a man — who has deceived
me, it is true — but who is poor, and older
than I, and a kind of a gentleman too.
On the whole, I prefer the massacre of
weeds.

Sunday.

When I had done talking to you yesterday, I played on my pipe till the conch
sounded, then went over to the old house
for dinner, and had scarce risen from table
ere I was submerged with visitors. The
first of these despatched, I spent the rest
of the evening going over the Samoan
translation of my *Bottle Imp* [1] with Claxton

---

[1] The first serial tale, says Mr. Clarke, ever read by
Samoans in their own language was the story of the *Bottle
Imp*, "which found its way into print at Samoa, and was
read with wonder and delight in many a thatched Samoan
hut before it won the admiration of readers at home."
In the English form the story was published first in *Black
and White*, and afterwards in the volume called *Island
Nights' Entertainments*.

the missionary; then to bed, but being upset, I suppose, by these interruptions, and having gone all day without my weeding, not to sleep. For hours I lay awake and heard the rain fall, and saw faint, far-away lightning over the sea, and wrote you long letters which I scorn to reproduce. This morning Paul was unusually early; the dawn had scarce begun when he appeared with the tray and lit my candle; and I had breakfasted and read (with indescribable sinkings) the whole of yesterday's work before the sun had risen. Then I sat and thought, and sat and better thought. It was not good enough, nor good; it was as slack as journalism, but not so inspired; it was excellent stuff misused, and the defects stood gross on it like humps upon a camel. But could I, in my present disposition, do much more with it? in my present pressure for time, were I not better employed doing another one about as ill, than making this some thousandth fraction better? Yes, I thought;

and tried the new one, and behold, I could
do nothing: my head swims, words do not
come to me, nor phrases, and I accepted
defeat, packed up my traps, and turned to
communicate the failure to my esteemed
correspondent.   I think it possible I over-
worked yesterday.   Well, we 'll see to-
morrow — perhaps try again later.   It is
indeed the hope of trying later that keeps
me writing to you.   If I take to my pipe,
I know myself — all is over for the morning.   Hurray, I 'll correct proofs!

Pago-Pago, Wednesday.

After I finished on Sunday I passed a
miserable day; went out weeding, but
could not find peace.   I do not like to
steal my dinner, unless I have given myself a holiday in a canonical manner; and
weeding after all is only fun, the amount
of its utility small, and the thing capable
of being done faster and nearly as well by
a hired boy.   In the evening Sewall came
up (American consul) and proposed to

take me on a malaga,[1] which I accepted.
Monday I rode down to Apia, was nearly
all day fighting about drafts and money;
the silver problem does not touch you, but
it is (in a strange and I hope passing
phase) making my situation difficult in
Apia. About eleven, the flags were all
half-masted; it was old Captain Hamilton
(Samesoni the natives called him) who had
passed away. In the evening I walked
round to the U. S. Consulate; it was a
lovely night with a full moon; and as I
got round to the hot corner of Matautu I
heard hymns in front. The balcony of the
dead man's house was full of women singing; Mary (the widow, a native) sat on a
chair by the doorstep, and I was set beside
her on a bench, and next to Paul the
carpenter; as I sat down I had a glimpse
of the old captain, who lay in a sheet on
his own table. After the hymn was over,
a native pastor made a speech which lasted
a long while; the light poured out of the

1 Boating expedition.

door and windows; the girls were sitting
clustered at my feet; it was choking hot.
After the speech was ended, Mary carried
me within; the captain's hands were folded
on his bosom, his face and head were composed; he looked as if he might speak at
any moment; I have never seen this kind
of waxwork so express or more venerable;
and when I went away, I was conscious of
a certain envy for the man who was out of
the battle.   All night it ran in my head,
and the next day when we sighted Tutuila,
and ran into this beautiful land-locked
loch of Pago-Pago (whence I write), Captain
Hamilton's folded hands and quiet face
said a great deal more to me than the
scenery.

I am living here in a trader's house; we
have a good table, Sewall doing things in
style; and I hope to benefit by the change,
and possibly get more stuff for Letters.
In the meanwhile, I am seized quite *mal-à-
propos* with desire to write a story, *The
Bloody Wedding*, founded on fact — very

possibly true, being an attempt to read a murder case — not yet months old, in this very place and house where I now write. The indiscretion is what stops me; but if I keep on feeling as I feel just now it will have to be written. Three Star Nettison, Kit Nettison, Field the Sailor, these are the main characters: old Nettison, and the captain of the man of war, the secondary. Possible scenario. Chapter I. . . .

VII

1891
April.

My Dear Colvin, — I got back on Monday night, after twenty-three hours in an open boat; the keys were lost; the Consul (who had promised us a bottle of Burgundy) nobly broke open his store-room, and we got to bed about midnight. Next morning the blessed Consul promised us horses for the daybreak; forgot all about it, worthy man; set us off at last in the heat of the day, and by a short cut which caused infinite trouble, and we were not home till dinner. I was extenuated, and have had a high fever since, or should have been writing before. To-day for the first time, I risk it. Tuesday I was pretty bad; Wednesday had a fever to kill a horse; Thursday I was better, but still out of ability to do aught but read awful trash. This is the time one misses civilisation; I wished to send out for some police novels;

Montépin would have about suited my
frozen brain.   It is a bother when all one's
thought turns on one's work in some sense
or other; I could not even think yesterday;
I took to inventing dishes by way of enter-
tainment.   Yesterday, while I lay asleep
in the afternoon, a very lucky thing happened; the Chief Justice came to call; met
one of our employés on the road; and was
shown what I had done to the road.

"Is this the road across the island?" he
asked.

"The only one," said Innes.

"And has one man done all this?"

"Three times," said the trusty Innes.
"It has had to be made three times, and
when Mr. Stevenson came, it was a track
like what you see beyond."

"This must be put right," said the Chief
Justice.

Sunday.

The truth is, I broke down yesterday
almost as soon as I began, and have been
surreptitiously finishing the entry to-day.

For all that I was much better, ate all the
time, and had no fever. The day was
otherwise uneventful. I am reminded; I
had another visitor on Friday; and Fanny
and Lloyd, as they returned from a forest
raid, met in our desert, untrodden road,
first Father Didier, Keeper of the conscience of Mataafa, the rising star; and
next the Chief Justice, sole stay of Laupepa,
the present and unsteady star, and remember, a few days before we were close to
the sick bed and entertained by the amateur
physician of Tamasese, the late and sunken
star. "That is the fun of this place,"
observed Lloyd; "everybody you meet is
so important." Everybody is also so
gloomy. It will come to war again, is
the opinion of all the well informed — and
before that to many bankruptcies; and
after that, as usual, to famine. Here,
under the microscope, we can see history
at work.

Wednesday.

I have been very neglectful. A return 1891 April. to work, perhaps premature, but necessary, has used up all my possible energies and made me acquainted with the living headache. I just jot down some of the past notabilia. Yesterday B., a carpenter, and K., my (unsuccessful) white man, were absent all morning from their work; I was working myself, where I hear every sound with morbid certainty, and I can testify that not a hammer fell. Upon inquiry I found they had passed the morning making ice with our ice machine and taking the horizon with a spirit level! I had no sooner heard this than — a violent headache set in; I am a real employer of labour now, and have much of the ship captain when aroused; and if I had a headache, I believe both these gentlemen had aching hearts. I promise you, the late —— was to the front; and K., who was the most guilty, yet (in a sense) the least blamable, having the brains and character of a canary-

bird, fared none the better for B.'s rep-
artees. I hear them hard at work this
morning, so the menace may be blessed.
It was just after my dinner, just before
theirs, that I administered my redoubtable
tongue — it is really redoubtable — to these
skulkers. (Paul used to truimph over Mr.
J. for weeks. "I am very sorry for you,"
he would say; "you're going to have a
talk with Mr. Stevenson when he comes
home: you don't know what that is!") In
fact, none of them do, till they get it. I
have known K., for instance, for months;
he has never heard me complain, or take
notice, unless it were to praise; I have
used him always as my guest, and there
seems to be something in my appearance
which suggests endless, ovine long-suffer-
ing! We sat in the upper verandah all
evening, and discussed the price of iron
roofing, and the state of the draught-horses,
with Innes, a new man we have taken, and
who seems to promise well.

One thing embarrasses me. No one

ever seems to understand my attitude about that book; the stuff sent was never meant for other than a first state; I never meant it to appear as a book.   Knowing well that I have never had one hour of inspiration since it was begun, and have only beaten out my metal by brute force and patient repetition, I hoped some day to get a "spate of style" and burnish it — fine mixed metaphor.   I am now so sick that I intend, when the Letters are done and some more written that will be wanted, simply to make a book of it by the pruning-knife.   I cannot fight longer; I am sensible of having done worse than I hoped, worse than I feared; all I can do now is to do the best I can for the future, and clear the book, like a piece of bush, with axe and cutlass.   Even to produce the MS. of this will occupy me, at the most favourable opinion, till the middle of next year; really five years were wanting, when I could have made a book; but I have a family and — perhaps I could not make the book after all.

VIII

MY DEAR COLVIN, — I begin again. I was awake this morning about half-past four. It was still night, but I made my fire, which is always a deligthful employment, and read Lockhart's "Scott" until the day began to peep. It was a beautiful and sober dawn, a dove-coloured dawn, insensibly brightening to gold. I was looking at it some while over the downhill profile of our eastern road, when I chanced to glance northward, and saw with extraordinary pleasure the sea lying outspread. It seemed as smooth as glass, and yet I knew the surf was roaring all along the reef, and indeed, if I had listened, I could have heard it — and saw the white sweep of it outside Matautu.

I am out of condition still, and can do nothing, and toil to be at my pen, and see some ink behind me. I have taken up again *The High Woods of Ulufanua.* I still think the fable too fantastic and far-fetched. But, on a re-reading, fell in love with my first chapter, and for good or evil I must finish it. It is really good, well fed with facts, true to the manners, and (for once in my works) rendered pleasing by the presence of a heroine who is pretty. Miss Uma is pretty; a fact. All my other women have been as ugly as sin, and like Falconet's horse (I have just been reading the anecdote in Lockhart), *mortes* forbye.

News: Our old house is now half demolished; it is to be rebuilt on a new site; now we look down upon and through the open posts of it like a bird-cage, to the woods beyond. My poor Paulo has lost his father and succeeded to thirty thousand thalers (I think); he had to go down to the Consulate yesterday to send a legal paper; got drunk, of course, and is still this morning in so bemused a condition that our breakfasts all went wrong. Lafaele is

absent at the deathbed of his fair spouse;
fair she was, but not in deed, acting as
harlot to the wreckers at work on the war-
ships, to which society she probably owes
her end, having fallen off a cliff, or been
thrust off it — *inter pocula.* Henry is the
same, our stand-by. In this transition
stage he has been living in Apia; but the
other night he stayed up, and sat with us
about the chimney in my room. It was
the first time he had seen a fire in a hearth;
he could not look at it without smiles, and
was always anxious to put on another stick.
We entertained him with the fairy tales of
civilisation — theatres, London, blocks in
the street, Universities, the Underground,
newspapers, etc., and projected once more
his visit to Sydney. If we can manage, it
will be next Christmas. (I see it will
be impossible for me to afford a further
journey *this* winter.) We have spent since
we have been here about £2500, which is
not much if you consider we have built on
that three houses, one of them of some

size, and a considerable stable, made two miles of road some three times, cleared many acres of bush, made some miles of path, planted quanities of food, and enclosed a horse paddock and some acres of pig run; but 't is a good deal of money regarded simply as money. K. is bosh; I have no use for him; but we must do what we can with the fellow meanwhile; he is good-humoured and honest, but inefficient, idle himself, the cause of idleness in others, grumbling, a self-excuser — all the faults in a bundle. He owes us thirty weeks' service — the wretched Paul about half as much. Henry is almost the only one of our employés who has a credit.

May 17th.

Well, am I ashamed of myself? I do not think so. I have been hammering Letters ever since, and got three ready and a fourth about half through; all four will go by the mail, which is what I wish, for so I keep at least my start. Days and

days of unprofitable stubbing and digging,
and the result still poor as literature, left-
handed, heavy, unillumined, but I believe
readable and interesting as matter. It has
been no joke of a hard time, and when my
task was done, I had little taste for anything but blowing on the pipe. A few
necessary letters filled the bowl to over-
flowing.

My mother has arrived, young, well, and
in good spirits. By desperate exertions,
which have wholly floored Fanny, her
room was ready for her, and the dining-
room fit to eat in. It was a famous vic-
tory. Lloyd never told me of your portrait
till a few days ago; fortunately, I had no
pictures hung yet; and the space over my
chimney waits your counterfeit present-
ment. I have not often heard anything
that pleased me more; your severe head
shall frown upon me and keep me to the
mark. But why has it not come? Have
you been as forgetful as Lloyd?

18*th.*

Miserable comforters are ye all! I read your esteemed pages this morning by lamp-light and the glimmer of the dawn, and as soon as breakfast was over, I must turn to and tackle these despised labours! Some courage was necessary, but not wanting. There is one thing at least by which I can avenge myself for my drubbing, for on one point you seem impenetrably stupid. Can I find no form of words which will at last convey to your intelligence the fact that *these letters were never meant, and are not now meant, to be other than a quarry of materials from which the book may be drawn?* There seems something incommunicable in this (to me) simple idea; I know Lloyd failed to comprehend it, I doubt if he has grasped it now; and I despair, after all these efforts, that you should ever be enlightened. Still, oblige me by reading that form of words once more, and see if a light does not break. You may be sure, after the friendly freedoms of your criti-

cism (necessary I am sure, and wholesome
I know, but untimely to the poor labourer
in his landslip) that mighty little of it
will stand.

Our Paul has come into a fortune, and
wishes to go home to the Hie Germanie.
This is a tile on our head, and if a shower,
which is now falling, lets up, I must go
down to Apia, and see if I can find a substitute of any kind. This is, from any
point of view, disgusting; above all, from
that of work; for whatever the result, the
mill has to be kept turning; apparently
dust, and not flour, is the proceed. Well,
there is gold in the dust, which is a fine
consolation, since — well, I can't help it;
night or morning, I do my darndest, and
if I cannot charge for merit, I must e'en
charge for toil, of which I have plenty and
plenty more ahead before this cup is
drained; sweat and hyssop are the in-
gredients.

We are clearing from Carruthers' Road
to the pig fence. Twenty-eight powerful

natives with Catholic medals about their
necks, all swiping in like Trojans; long may the sport continue!

The invoice to hand. Ere this goes out, I hope to see your expressive, but surely not benignant countenance! Adieu, O culler of offensive expressions — " and a' to be a posy to your ain dear May!" — Fanny seems a little revived again after her spasm of work. Our books and furniture keep slowly draining up the road, in a sad state of scatterment and disrepair; I wish the devil had had K. by his red beard before he had packed my library. Odd leaves and sheets and boards — a thing to make a bibliomaniac shed tears — are fished out of odd corners. But I am no bibliomaniac, praise Heaven, and I bear up, and rejoice when I find anything safe.

19th.

However, I worked five hours on the brute, and finished my Letter all the same, and could n't sleep last night by consequence. Have n't had a bad night since I

don't know when; dreamed a large, handsome man (a New Orleans planter) had
insulted my wife, and, do what I pleased,
I could not make him fight me; and woke
to find it was the eleventh anniversary of
my marriage. A letter usually takes me
from a week to three days; but I 'm sometimes two days on a page — I was once
three — and then my friends kick me.
C'est-y-bête! I wish letters of that charming quality could be so timed as to arrive
when a fellow was n't working at the truck
in question; but, of course, that can't be.
Did not go down last night. It showered
all afternoon, and poured heavy and loud
all night.

You should have seen our twenty-five
popes (the Samoan phrase for a Catholic,
lay or cleric) squatting when the day's
work was done on the ground outside the
verandah, and pouring in the rays of forty-
eight eyes through the back and the front
door of the dining-room, while Henry and
I and the boss pope signed the contract.

The second boss (an old man) wore a kilt (as usual) and a Balmoral bonnet with a little tartan edging and the tails pulled off. I told him that hat belonged to my country — Sekotia; and he said, yes, that was the place that he belonged to right enough. And then all the Papists laughed till the woods rang; he was slashing away with a cutlass as he spoke.

The pictures have decidedly not come; they may probably arrive Sunday.

IX

1891
June.
Sir, — To you, under your portrait,
which is, in expression, your true, breath-
ing self, and up to now saddens me; in
time, and soon, I shall be glad to have it
there; it is still only a reminder of your
absence. Fanny wept when we unpacked
it, and you know how little she is given to
that mood; I was scarce Roman myself,
but that does not count — I lift up my
voice so readily. These are good compli-
ments to the artist. I write in the midst
of a wreck of books, which have just come
up, and have for once defied my labours to
get straight. The whole floor is filled
with them, and (what's worse) most of the
shelves forbye; and where they are to go
to, and what is to become of the librarian,
God knows. It is hot to-night, and has
been airless all day, and I am out of sorts,
and my work sticks, the devil fly away

with it and me.   We had an alarm of war
since last I wrote my screeds to you, and
it blew over, and is to blow on again, and
the rumour goes they are to begin by kill-
ing all the whites.   I have no belief in
this, and should be infinitely sorry if it
came to pass — I do not mean for *us*, that
were otiose — but for the poor, deluded
schoolboys, who should hope to gain by
such a step.

[*Letter resumed.*]

June 20th.

No diary this time.   Why? you ask.   I
have only sent out four Letters, and two
chapters of the *Wrecker.*   Yes, but to get
these I have written 132 pp., 66,000 words
in thirty days; 2200 words a day; the
labours of an elephant.   God knows what
it 's like, and don't ask me, but nobody
shall say I have spared pains.   I thought
for some time it would n't come at all.   I
was days and days over the first letter of
the lot — days and days writing and delet-
ing and making no headway whatever, till

I thought I should have gone bust; but it came at last after a fashion, and the rest went a thought more easily, though I am not so fond as to fancy any better.

Your opinion as to the letters as a whole is so damnatory that I put them by. But there is a "hell of a want of" money this year. And these Gilbert Island papers, being the most interesting in matter, and forming a compact whole, and being well illustrated, I did think of as a possible resource.

It would be called

Six Months in Melanesia,
Two Island Kings,
————*Monarchies,*
Gilbert Island Kings,
————*Monarchies,*

and I daresay I 'll think of a better yet — and would divide thus : —

Butaritari.

  I. A Town asleep.
  II. The Three Brothers.

I wish you to watch these closely, judging them as a whole, and treating them as I have asked you, and favour me with your damnatory advice. I look up at your portrait, and it frowns upon me. You seem to view me with reproach. The expression is excellent; Fanny wept when she

saw it, and you know she is not given to
the melting mood. She seems really
better; I have a touch of fever again, I
fancy overwork, and to-day, when I have
overtaken my letters, I shall blow on my
pipe. Tell Mrs. S. I have been playing
Le Chant d' Amour lately, and have arranged
it, after awful trouble, rather prettily for
two pipes; and it brought her before me
with an effect scarce short of hallucination.
I could hear her voice in every note; yet I
had forgot the air entirely, and began to
pipe it from notes as something new, when
I was brought up with a round turn by this
reminiscence. We are now very much
installed; the dining-room is done, and
looks lovely. Soon we shall begin to photograph and send you our circumstances.
My room is still a howling wilderness. I
sleep on a platform in a window, and strike
my mosquito bar and roll up my bedclothes
every morning, so that the bed becomes by
day a divan. A great part of the floor is
knee-deep in books, yet nearly all the

shelves are filled, alas! It is a place to make a pig recoil, yet here are my interminable labours begun daily by lamp-light, and sometimes not yet done when the lamp has once more to be lighted. The effect of pictures in this place is surprising. They give great pleasure.

June 21st.

A word more. I had my breakfast this morning at 4.30! My new cook has beaten me and (as Lloyd says) revenged all the cooks in the world. I have been hunting them to give me breakfast early since I was twenty; and now here comes Mr. Ratke, and I have to plead for mercy. I cannot stand 4.30; I am a mere fevered wreck; it is now half-past eight, and I can no more, and four hours divide me from lunch, the devil take the man! Yesterday it was about 5.30, which I can stand; day before 5, which is bad enough; to-day, I give out. It is like a London season, and as I do not take a siesta once in a month, and then only five minutes, I am being worn to the bones, and look aged and anxious.

We have Rider Haggard's brother here as a Land Commissioner; a nice kind of a fellow; indeed, all the three Land Commssioners are very agreeable.

X

MY DEAR COLVIN,[1] — Yours from Loch-
inver has just come. You ask me if I am
ever homesick for the Highlands and the
Isles. Conceive that for the last month I
have been living there between 1786 and
1850, in my grandfather's diaries and
letters. I *had* to take a rest; no use
talking; so I put in a month over my *Lives
of the Stevensons* with great pleasure and
profit and some advance; one chapter and
a part drafted. The whole promises well.
Chapter I. Domestic Annals. Capter II.
The Northern Lights. Chapter III. The
Bell Rock. Chapter IV. A Family of
Boys. Chap. V. The Grandfather. VI.

---

[1] Between this letter and the preceding, one has gone
astray. It was chiefly concerned with the disturbed state
of Samoan affairs, the threatenings of war, and the mis-
management of the two treaty officials.

Alan Stevenson. VII. Thomas Stevenson.
My materials for my great-grandfather are
almost null; for my grandfather copious
and excellent. Name, a puzzle. *A Scottish
Family*, *A Family of Engineers*, *Northern
Lights*, *The Engineers of the Northern
Lights: A Family History*. Advise; but
it will take long. Now, imagine if I have
been homesick for Barrahead and Island
Glass, and Kirkwall, and Cape Wrath, and
the Wells of the Pentland Firth; I could
have wept.

Now for politics. I am much less
alarmed; I believe the *malo* (= *raj*, government) will collapse and cease like an over-
lain infant, without a shot fired. They
have now been months here on their big
salaries — and Cedarcrantz, whom I specially like as a man, has done nearly nothing, and the Baron, who is well-meaning,
has done worse. They have these large
salaries, and they have all the taxes; they
have made scarce a foot of road; they have
not given a single native a position — all

to white men; they have scarce laid out a
penny on Apia, and scarce a penny on
the King; they have forgot they were in
Samoa, or that such a thing as Samoans
existed, and had eyes and some intelligence. The Chief Justice has refused to
pay his customs! The President proposed
to have an expensive house built for himself, while the King, his master, has none!
I had stood aside, and been a loyal, and,
above all, a silent subject, up to then; but
now I snap my fingers at their *malo*. It is
damned, and I 'm damned glad of it. And
this is not all. Last *" Wainiu,"* when I
sent Fanny off to Fiji, I hear the wonderful news that the Chief Justice is going to
Fiji and the Colonies to improve his mind.
I showed my way of thought to his guest,
Count Wachtmeister, whom I have sent to
you with a letter — he will tell you all the
news. Well, the Chief Justice stayed, but
they said he was to leave yesterday. I
had intended to go down, and see and warn
him! But the President's house had come

up in the meanwhile, and I let them go to their doom, which I am only anxious to see swiftly and (if it may be) bloodlessly fall.

Thus I have in a way withdrawn my unrewarded loyalty. Lloyd is down to-day with Moors to call on Mataafa; the news of the excursion made a considerable row in Apia, and both the German and the English consuls besought Lloyd not to go. But he stuck to his purpose, and with my approval. It's a poor thing if people are to give up a pleasure party for a *malo* that has never done anything for us but draw taxes, and is going to go pop, and leave us at the mercy of the identical Mataafa, whom I have not visited for more than a year, and who is probably furious.

The sense of my helplessness here has been rather bitter; I feel it wretched to see this dance of folly and injustice and unconscious rapacity go forward from day to day, and to be impotent. I was not consulted — or only by one man, and that

on particular points; I did not choose to
volunteer advice till some pressing occasion; I have not even a vote, for I am not a member of the municipality.

What ails you, miserable man, to talk of saving material? I have a whole world in my head, a whole new society to work, but I am in no hurry; you will shortly make the acquaintance of the Island of Ulufanua, on which I mean to lay several stories; the *Bloody Wedding*, possibly the *High Woods* — (Oh, it 's so good, the High Woods, but the story is craziness; that 's the trouble,) — a political story, the *Labour Slave*, etc. Ulufanua is an imaginary island; the name is a beautiful Samoan word for the *top* of a forest; ulu — leaves or hair, fanua = land. The ground or country of the leaves. "Ulufanua the isle of the sea," read that verse dactylically and you get the beat; the *u's* are like our double *oo*; did ever you hear a prettier word?

I do not feel inclined to make a volume

of Essays,[1] but if I did, and perhaps the idea is good — and any idea is better than South Seas — here would be my choice of the Scribner articles: *Dreams*, *Beggars*, *Lantern-Bearers*, *Random Memories*. There was a paper called the *Old Pacific Capital* in Fraser, in Tulloch's time, which had merit; there were two on Fontainebleau in the *Magazine of Art* in Henley's time. I have no idea if they're any good; then there's the *Emigrant Train*. *Pulvis et Umbra* is in a different key, and would n't hang on with the rest.

I have just interrupted my letter and read through the chapter of the *High Woods* that is written, a chapter and a bit, some sixteen pages, really very fetching, but what do you wish? the story is so wilful, so steep, so silly — it's a hallucination I have outlived, and yet I never did a better piece of work, horrid, and pleasing,

---

[1] In reply to a suggestion which ultimately took effect in the shape of the volume called *Across the Plains* (Chatto and Windus, 1892).

and extraordinarily *true;* it 's sixteen pages of the South Seas; their essence. What am I to do? Lose this little gem — for I 'll be bold, and that 's what I think it — or go on with the rest, which I don't believe in, and don't like, and which can never make aught but a silly yarn? Make another end to it? Ah, yes, but that 's not the way I write; the whole tale is implied; I never use an effect when I can help it, unless it prepares the effects that are to follow; that 's what a story consists in. To make another end, that is to make the beginning all wrong. The dénouement of a long story is nothing; it is just a "full close," which you may approach and accompany as you please — it is a coda, not an essential member in the rhythm; but the body and end of a short story is bone of the bone and blood of the blood of the beginning. Well, I shall end by finishing it against my judgment; that fragment is my Delilah. Golly, it 's good. I am not shining by modesty; but I do just love the

colour and movement of that piece so far as
it goes.

I was surprised to hear of your fishing.
And you saw the "Pharos," [1] thrice fortunate man; I wish I dared go home, I would
ask the Commissioners to take me round
for old sake's sake, and see all my family
pictures once more from the Mull of Gal-
loway to Unst.   However, all is arranged
for our meeting in Ceylon, except the date
and the blooming pounds.   I have heard of
an exquisite hotel in the country, airy,
large rooms, good cookery, not dear; we
shall have a couple of months there, if we
can make it out, and converse or — as
my grandfather always said — "commune."
"Communings with Mr. Kennedy as to
Lighthouse Repairs."   He was a fine old
fellow, but a droll.

[1] The steam-yacht of the Commissioners of Northern
Lights, on which he had been accustomed as a lad to
accompany his father on the official trips of inspection
round the coast.

Evening.

Lloyd has returned. Peace and war
were played before his eyes at heads or
tails. A German was stopped with levelled
guns; he raised his whip; had it fallen,
we might have been now in war. Excuses
were made by Mataafa himself. Doubtless the thing was done — I mean the stop-
ping of the German — a little to show off
before Lloyd. Meanwhile —— was up
here, telling how the Chief Justice was
really gone for five or eight weeks, and
begging me to write to the *Times* and
denounce the state of affairs; many strong
reasons he advanced; and Lloyd and I have
been since his arrival and ——'s departure,
near half an hour, debating what should be
done. Cedarcrantz is gone; it is not my
fault; he knows my views on that point —
alone of all points; — he leaves me with
my mouth sealed. Yet this is a nice thing
that because he is guilty of a fresh offence
— his flight — the mouth of the only
possible influential witness should be

closed! I do not like this argument. I look like a cad, if I do in the man's absence what I could have done in a more manly manner in his presence. True; but why did he go? It is his last sin. And I, who like the man extremely — that is the word — I love his society — he is intelligent, pleasant, even witty, a gentleman — and you know how that attaches — I loathe to seem to play a base part; but the poor natives — who are like other folk, false enough, lazy enough, not heroes, not saints — ordinary men damnably misused — are they to suffer because I like Cedarcrantz, and Cedarcrantz has cut his lucky? This is a little tragedy, observe well — a tragedy! I may be right, I may be wrong in my judgment, but I am in treaty with my honour. I know not how it will seem to-morrow. Lloyd thought the barrier of honour insurmountable, and it is an ugly obstacle. He (Cedarcrantz) will likely meet my wife three days from now, may travel back with her, will be charming if he does; suppose this, and suppose him to arrive and find that I have sprung a mine — or the nearest approach to it I could find — behind his back? My position is pretty. Yes, I am an aristocrat. I have the old petty, personal view of honour? I should blush till I die if I do this; yet it is on the cards that I may do it. So much I have written you in bed, as a man writes, or talks, in a *bittre Wahl.* Now I shall sleep, and see if I am more clear. I will consult the missionaries at least — I place some reliance in M. also — or I should if he were not a partisan; but a partisan he is. There 's the pity. To sleep! A fund of wisdom in the prostrate body and the fed brain. Kindly observe R. L. S. in the talons of politics! 'Tis funny — 't is sad. Nobody but these cursed idiots could have so driven me; I cannot bear idiots.

My dear Colvin, I must go to sleep; it is long past ten — a dreadful hour for me. And here am I lingering (so I feel) in the dining-room at the Monument, talking to

you across the table, both on our feet, and
only the two stairs to mount, and get to
bed, and sleep, and be waked by dear old
George — to whom I wish my kindest
remembrances — next morning.   I look
round, and there is my blue room, and my
long lines of shelves, and the door gaping
on a moonless night, and no word of S. C.
but his twa portraits on the wall.   Good-
bye, my dear fellow, and good-night.
Queer place the world!

Monday.

No clearness of mind with the morning;
I have no guess what I should do.   'T is
easy to say that the public duty should
brush aside these little considerations of
personal dignity; so it is that politicians
begin, and in a month you find them rat
and flatter and intrigue with brows of
brass.   I am rather of the old view, that a
man's first duty is to these little laws; the
big he does not, he never will understand;
I may be wrong about the Chief Justice

and the Baron and the state of Samoa; I
cannot be wrong about the vile attitude I put myself in if I blow the gaff on Cedar-crantz behind his back.

Tuesday.

One more word about the South Seas, in answer to a question I observe I have forgotten to answer. The Tahiti part has never turned up, because it has never been written. As for telling you where I went or when, or anything about Honolulu, I would rather die; that is fair and plain. How can anybody care when or how I left Honolulu? A man of upwards of forty cannot waste his time in communicating matter of that indifference. The letters, it appears, are tedious; they would be more tedious still if I wasted my time upon such infantile and sucking-bottle details. If ever I put in any such detail, it is because it leads into something or serves as a transition. To tell it for its own sake, never! The mistake is all

through that I have told too much; I had
not sufficient confidence in the reader, and
have overfed him; and here are you anxious
to learn how I — O Colvin! Suppose it
had made a book, all such information is
given to one glance of an eye by a map
with a little dotted line upon it. But let
us forget this unfortunate affair.

Wednesday.

Yesterday I went down to consult Clarke,
who took the view of delay. Has he
changed his mind already? I wonder:
here at least is the news. Some little
while back some men of Manono — what
is Manono? — a Samoan rotten borough,
a small isle of huge political importance,
heaven knows why, where a handful of
chiefs make half the trouble in the country.
Some men of Manono (which is strong
Mataafa) burned down the houses and destroyed the crops of some Malietoa neighbours. The President went there the other
day and landed alone on the island, which

(to give him his due) was plucky. Moreover, he succeeded in persuading the folks
to come up and be judged on a particular
day in Apia. That day they did not come;
but did come the next, and to their vast
surprise, were given six months' imprison-
ment and clapped in gaol. Those who had
accompanied them, cried to them on the
streets as they were marched to prison,
"Shall we rescue you?" The condemned,
marching in the hands of thirty men with
loaded rifles, cried out "No!" And the
trick was done. But it was ardently believed a rescue would be attempted; the
gaol was laid about with armed men day
and night; but there was some question of
their loyalty, and the commandant of the
forces, a very nice young beardless Swede,
became nervous, and conceived a plan.
How if he should put dynamite under the
gaol, and in case of an attempted rescue
blow up prison and all? He went to the
President, who agreed; he went to the
American man-of-war for the dynamite

and machine, was refused, and got it at last from the Wreckers. The thing began to leak out, and there arose a muttering in town. People had no fancy for amateur explosions, for one thing. For another, it did not clearly appear that it was legal; the men had been condemned to six months' prison, which they were peaceably undergoing; they had not been condemned to death. And lastly, it seemed a somewhat advanced example of civilisation to set before barbarians. The mutter in short became a storm, and yesterday, while I was down, a cutter was chartered, and the prisoners were suddenly banished to the Tokelaus. Who has changed the sentence? We are going to stir in the dynamite matter; we do not want the natives to fancy us consenting to such an outrage.[1]

Fanny has returned from her trip, and on the whole looks better. The *High*

---

[1] More about this affair is to be found in the writer's letters of the same date to the *Times*, and in his *Footnote to History*, p. 297.

Woods are under way, and their name is 1891 Sept. now the *Beach of Falesá*, and the yarn is cured. I have about thirty pages of it done; it will be fifty to seventy I suppose. No supernatural trick at all; and escaped out of it quite easily; can't think why I was so stupid for so long. Mighty glad to have Fanny back to this "Hell of the South Seas," as the German Captain called it. What will Cedarcrantz think when he comes back? To do him justice, had he been here, this Manono hash would not have been.

Here is a pretty thing. When Fanny was in Fiji all the Samoa and Toeklau folks were agog about our "flash" house; but the whites had never heard of it.

ROBERT LOUIS STEVENSON,
Author of *The Beach of Falesá.*

XI.

MY DEAR COLVIN, — Since I last laid
down my pen, I have written and rewritten
The Beach of Falesá; something like sixty
thousand words of sterling domestic fiction
(the story, you will understand, is only
half that length); and now I don't want to
write any more again for ever, or feel so;
and I 've got to overhaul it once again to
my sorrow. I was all yesterday revising,
and found a lot of slacknesses and (what is
worse in this kind of thing) some literary-
isms. One of the puzzles is this: It is a
first person story — a trader telling his own
adventure in an island. When I began I
allowed myself a few liberties, because I
was afraid of the end; now the end proved
quite easy, and could be done in the pace;
so the beginning remains about a quarter
tone out (in places); but I have rather

decided to let it stay so. The problem is always delicate; it is the only thing that worries me in first person tales, which otherwise (quo' Alan) "set better wi' my genius." There is a vast deal of fact in the story, and some pretty good comedy. It is the first realistic South Sea story; I mean with real South Sea character and details of life. Everybody else who has tried, that I have seen, got carried away by the romance, and ended in a kind of sugar-candy sham epic, and the whole effect was lost — there was no etching, no human grin, consequently no conviction. Now I have got the smell and look of the thing a good deal. You will know more about the South Seas after you have read my little tale than if you had read a library. As to whether any one else will read it, I have no guess. I am in an off time, but there is just the possibility it might make a hit; for the yarn is good and melodra-matic, and there is quite a love affair — for me; and Mr. Wiltshire (the narrator) is a huge lark, though I say it. But there is always the exotic question, and everything, the life, the place, the dialects — trader's talk, which is a strange conglomerate of literary expressions and English and American slang, and Beach de Mar, or native English, — the very trades and hopes and fears of the characters, are all novel, and may be found unwelcome to that great, hulking, bullering whale, the public.

Since I wrote, I have been likewise drawing up a document to send it to the President; it has been dreadfully delayed, not by me, but to-day they swear it will be sent in. A list of questions about the dynamite report are herein laid before him, and considerations suggested why he should answer.

October 5th.

Ever since my last snatch I have been much chivied about over the President business; his answer has come, and is an evasion accompanied with schoolboy inso-

lence, and we are going to try to answer
it. I drew my answer and took it down
yesterday; but one of the signatories wants
another paragraph added, which I have not
yet been able to draw, and as to the wisdom
of which I am not yet convinced.

1891
Oct.

Next day, Oct. 7th, the right day.

We are all in rather a muddled state
with our President affair. I do loathe
politics, but at the same time, I cannot
stand by and have the natives blown in the
air treacherously with dynamite. They
are still quiet; how long this may continue
I do not know, though of course by mere
prescription the Government is strengthened, and is probably insured till the next
taxes fall due. But the ·unpopularity of
the whites is growing. My native overseer, the great Henry Simelé, announced
to-day that he was "weary of whites upon
the beach. All too proud," said this vera-
cious witness. One of the proud ones had
threatened yesterday to cut off his head

with a bush knife! These are "native out-
rages;" honour bright, and setting theft
aside, in which the natives are active, this
is the main stream of irritation. The
natives are generally courtly, far from
always civil, but really gentle, and with a
strong sense of honour of their own, and
certainly quite as much civilised as our
dynamiting President.

We shall be delighted to see Kipling.[1]
I go to bed usually about half-past eight,
and my lamp is out before ten; I breakfast
at six. We may say roughly we have no
soda water on the island, and just now
truthfully no whisky. I *have* heard the
chimes at midnight; now no more, I guess.
But — Fanny and I, as soon as we can get
coins for it, are coming to Europe, not to
England: I am thinking of Royat. Bar
wars. If not, perhaps the Apennines
might give us a mountain refuge for two

---

[1] Mr. Rudyard Kipling was at this time planning a trip
to Samoa, but the plan was unfortunately not carried out,
and he and Stenvenson never met.

months or three in summer. How is that for high? But the money must be all in hand first.

October 13th.

How am I to describe my life these last few days? I have been wholly swallowed up in politics, a wretched business, with fine elements of farce in it too, which repay a man in passing, involving many dark and many moonlight rides, secret councils which are at once divulged, sealed letters which are read aloud in confidence to the neighbours, and a mass of fudge and fun, which would have driven me crazy ten years ago, and now makes me smile.

On Friday, Henry came and told us he must leave and go to "my poor old family in Savaii;" why? I do not quite know — but I suspect to be tattooed — if so, then probably to be married, and we shall see him no more. I told him he must do what he thought his duty; we had him to lunch, drank his health, and he and I rode down about twelve. When I got down, I sent

my horse back to help bring down the
family later. My own afternoon was cut
out for me; my last draft for the President
had been objected to by some of the signatories. I stood out, and one of our small
number accordingly refused to sign. Him
I had to go and persuade, which went off
very well after the first hottish moments;
you have no idea how stolid my temper is
now. By about five the thing was done;
and we sat down to dinner at the China-
man's — the Verrey or Doyen's of Apia —
G. and I at each end as hosts; G.'s wife
— Fanua, late maid of the village; her
(adopted) father and mother, Seumanu and
Faatulia, Fanny, Belle, Lloyd, Austin,
and Henry Simelé, his last appearance.
Henry was in a kilt of gray shawl, with a
blue jacket, white shirt and black necktie,
and looked like a dark genteel guest in a
Highland shooting-box. Seumanu (opposite Fanny, next G.) is chief of Apia, a
rather big gun in this place, looking like a
large, fatted, military Englishman, bar the

colour.   Faatulia, next me, is a bigger chief than her husband.   Henry is a chief too — his chief name, Iiga (Ee-eeng-a), he has not yet "taken" because of his youth. We were in fine society, and had a pleasant meal-time, with lots of fun.   Then to the Opera — I beg your pardon, I mean the Circus.   We occupied the first row in the reserved seats, and there in the row behind were all our friends — Captain Foss and his Captain-Lieutenant, three of the American officers, very nice fellows, the Dr., etc., so we made a fine show of what an embittered correspondent of the local paper called "the shoddy aristocracy of Apia;" and you should have seen how we carried on, and how I clapped, and Captain Foss hollered "*wunderschön!*" and threw himself forward in his seat, and how we all in fact enjoyed ourselves like school-children, Austin not a shade more than his neighbours.   Then the Circus broke up, and the party went home, but I stayed down, having business on the morrow.

Yesterday, October 12th, great news
reaches me, and Lloyd and I, with the
mail just coming in, must leave all, saddle,
and ride down. True enough, the President had resigned! Sought to resign his
presidency of the council, and keep his
advisership to the King; given way to the
Consul's objections and resigned all — then
fell out with them about the disposition of
the funds, and was now trying to resign
from his resignation! Sad little President,
so trim to look at, and I believe so kind to
his little wife! Not only so, but I meet
D. on the beach. D. calls me in consulta-
tion, and we make with infinite difficulty a
draft of a petition to the King. . . . Then
to dinner at M.'s, a very merry meal,
interrupted before it was over by the
arrival of the committee. Slight sketch
of procedure agreed upon, self-appointed
spokesman, and the deputation sets off.
Walk all through Matafele, all along
Mulinuu, come to the King's house; he
has verbally refused to see us in answer to

our letter, swearing he is gase-gase (chief-
sickness, not common man's), and indeed
we see him inside in bed.   It is a miserable
low house, better houses by the dozen in
the little hamlet (Tanugamanono) of bush-
men on our way to Vailima; and the
President's house in process of erection
just opposite! We are told to return to-
morrow; I refuse; and at last we are very
sourly received, sit on the mats, and I
open out, through a very poor interpreter,
and sometimes hampered by unacceptable
counsels from my backers. I can speak
fairly well in a plain way now. C. asked
me to write out my harangue for him this
morning; I have done so, and could n't get
it near as good. I suppose (talking and
interpreting) I was twenty minutes or half-
an-hour on the deck; then his majesty
replied in the dying whisper of a big chief;
a few words of rejoinder (approving), and
the deputation withdrew, rather well
satisfied.

A few days ago this intervention would

have been a deportable offence; not now, I bet; I would like them to try. A little way back along Mulinuu, Mrs. G. met us with her husband's horse; and he and she and Lloyd and I rode back in a heavenly moonlight. Here ends a chapter in the life of an island politician! Catch me at it again; 't is easy to go in, but it is not a pleasant trade. I have had a good team, as good as I could get on the beach; but what trouble even so, and what fresh troubles shaping. But I have on the whole carried all my points; I believe all but one, and on that (which did not concern me) I had no right to interfere. I am sure you would be amazed if you knew what a good hand I am at keeping my temper, talking people over, and giving reasons which are not my reasons, but calculated for the meridian of the particular objection; so soon does falsehood await the politician in his whirling path.

XII.

Monday, October 24th.

MY DEAR CARTHEW,[1] — See what I have
written, but it's Colvin I'm after — I have written two chapters, about thirty pages of *Wrecker* since the mail left, which must be my excuse, and the bother I've had with it is not to be imagined; you might have seen me the day before yesterday weighing British sov.'s and Chili dollars to arrange my treasure chest. And there was such a calculation, not for that only, but for the ship's position and distances when — but I am not going to tell you the yarn — and then, as my arithmetic is particularly lax, Lloyd had to go over all my calculations; and then, as I had changed the amount of money, he had to go over all *his* as to the

---

[1] Readers of the *Wrecker* will not need to be reminded that this is the name of the personage on whom the mystery in that story hinges.

amount of the lay; and altogether, a bank could be run with less effusion of figures than it took to shore up a single chapter of a measly yarn. However, it 's done, and I have but one more, or at the outside, two to do, and I am Free! and can do any damn thing I like.

Before falling on politics, I shall give you my day. Awoke somewhere about the first peep of day, came gradually to, and had a turn on the verandah before 5.55, when "the child" (an enormous Wallis Islander) brings me an orange; at 6, breakfast; 6.10, to work; which lasts till, at 10.30, Austin comes for his history lecture; this is rather dispiriting, but education must be gone about in faith — and charity, both of which pretty nigh failed me to-day about (of all things) Carthage; 11, luncheon; after luncheon in my mother's room, I read Chapter XXIII. of *The Wrecker*, then Belle, Lloyd, and I go up and make music furiously till about 2 (I suppose), when I turn into work again till 4; fool from 4 to half-past, tired out and waiting for the bath hour; 4.30, bath; 4.40, eat two heavenly mangoes on the verandah, and see the boys arrive with the pack-horses; 5, dinner; smoke, chat on verandah, then hand of cards, and at last at 8 come up to my room with a pint of beer and a hard biscuit, which I am now consuming, and as soon as they are consumed I shall turn in.

Such are the innocent days of this ancient and outworn sportsman; to-day there was no weeding, usually there is however, edged in somewhere. My books for the moment are a crib to Phædo, and the second book of Montaigne; and a little while back I was reading Frederic Harrison, "Choice of Books," etc. — very good indeed, a great deal of sense and knowledge in the volume, and some very true stuff, *contra* Carlyle, about the eighteenth century. A hideous idea came over me that perhaps Harrison is now getting *old*. Perhaps you are. Perhaps I am.

Oh, this infidelity must be stared firmly down. I am about twenty-three — say twenty-eight; you about thirty, or, by 'r lady, thirty-four; and as Harrison belongs to the same generation, there is no good bothering about him.

Here has just been a fine alert; I gave my wife a dose of chlorodyne. "Something wrong," says she. "Nonsense," said I. "Embrocation," said she. I smelt it, and — it smelt very funny. "I think it's just gone bad, and to-morrow will tell." Proved to be so.

Wednesday.

History of Tuesday. — Woke at usual time, very little work, for I was tired, and had a job for the evening — to write parts for a new instrument, a violin. Lunch, chat, and up to my place to practise; but there was no practising for me — my flageolet was gone wrong, and I had to take it all to pieces, clean it, and put it up again. As this is a most intricate job — the thing dissolves into seventeen separate members, most of these have to be fitted on their individual springs as fine as needles, and sometimes two at once with the springs shoving different ways — it took me till two. Then Lloyd and I rode forth on our errands; first to Motootua, where we had a really instructive conversation on weeds and grasses. Thence down to Apia, where we bought a fresh bottle of chlorodyne and conversed on politics.

My visit to the King, which I thought at the time a particularly nugatory and even schoolboy step, and only consented to because I had held the reins so tight over my little band before, has raised a deuce of a row — new proclamation, no one is to interview the sacred puppet without consuls' permission, two days' notice, and an approved interpreter — read (I suppose) spy. Then back; I should have said I was trying the new horse; a tallish piebald, bought from the circus; he proved steady and safe, but in very bad condition, and

not so much the wild Arab steed of the
desert as had been supposed. The height
of his back, after commodious Jack,
astonished me, and I had a great conscious-
ness of exercise and florid action, as I
posted to his long, emphatic trot. We had
to ride back easy; even so he was hot and
blown; and when we set a boy to lead him
to and fro, our last character for sanity
perished. We returned just neat for
dinner; and in the evening our violinist
arrived, a young lady, no great virtuoso
truly, but plucky, industrious, and a good
reader; and we played five pieces with
huge amusement, and broke up at nine.
This morning I have read a splendid piece
of Montaigne, written this page of letter,
and now turn to the *Wrecker*.

Wednesday — November 16th or 17th —
and I am ashamed to say mail day. The
Wrecker is finished, that is the best of my
news; it goes by this mail to Scribner's;
and I honestly think it a good yarn on the
whole and of its measly kind. The part

that is genuinely good is Nares, the American sailor; that is a genuine figure; had there been more Nares it would have been a better book; but of course it did n't set up to be a book, only a long tough yarn with some pictures of the manners of to-day in the greater world — not the shoddy sham world of cities, clubs, and colleges, but the world where men still live a man's life. The worst of my news is the influenza; Apia is devastate; the shops closed, a ball put off, etc. As yet we have not had it at Vailima, and who knows? we may escape. None of us go down, but of course the boys come and go.

Your letter had the most wonderful " I told you so " I ever heard in the course of my life. Why, you madman, I would n't change my present installation for any post, dignity, honour, or advantage conceivable to me. It fills the bill; I have the loveliest time. And as for wars and rumours of war, you surely know enough of me to be aware that I like that also a thou-

sand times better than decrepit peace in
Middlesex? I do not quite like politics;
I am too aristocratic, I fear, for that.
God knows I don't care who I chum with;
perhaps like sailors best; but to go round
and sue and sneak to keep a crowd together
— never. My imagination, which is not
the least damped by the idea of having my
head cut off in the bush, recoils aghast
from the idea of a life like Gladstone's,
and the shadow of the newspaper chills me
to the bone. Hence my late eruption was
interesting, but not what I like. All else
suits me in this (killed a mosquito) A1
abode.

About politics. A determination was
come to by the President that he had been
an idiot; emissaries came to G. and me to
kiss and be friends. My man proposed I
should have a personal interview; I said it
was quite useless, I had nothing to say; I
had offered him the chance to inform me,
had pressed it on him, and had been very
unpleasantly received, and now "Time

was." Then it was decided that I was to be made a culprit against Germany; the German Captain — a delightful fellow and our constant visitor — wrote to say that as "a German officer" he could not come even to say farewell. We all wrote back in the most friendly spirit, telling him (politely) that some of these days he would be sorry, and we should be delighted to see our friend again. Since then I have seen no German shadow.

Mataafa has been proclaimed a rebel; the President did this act, and then resigned. By singular good fortune, Mataafa has not yet moved; no thanks to our idiot governors. They have shot their bolt; they have made a rebel of the only man (*to their own knowledge, on the report of their own spy*) who held the rebel party in check; and having thus called on war to fall, they can do no more, sit equally "expertes" of *vis* and counsel, regarding their handiwork. It is always a cry with these folk that he (Mataafa) had no ammunition. I

always said it would be found; and we
know of five boat-loads that have found
their way to Malie already.   Where there
are traders, there will be ammunition;
aphorism by R. L. S.

Now what am I to do next?

Lives of the Stevensons? *Historia
Samoæ?* A History for Children? Fiction?
I have had two hard months at fiction;
I want a change.   Stevensons? I am
expecting some more material; perhaps
better wait.   Samoa; rather tempting;
might be useful to the islands — and to
me; for it will be written in admirable
temper; I have never agreed with any
party, and see merits and excuses in all;
should do it (if I did) very slackly and
easily, as if half in conversation.   History
for Children?   This flows from my lessons
to Austin; no book is any good.   The best
I have seen is Freeman's *Old English
History;* but his style is so rasping, and a
child can learn more, if he's clever.   I
found my sketch of general Aryan History,

given in conversation, to have been practically correct — at least what I mean is,
Freeman had very much the same stuff in
his early chapters, only not so much, and
I thought not so well placed; and the child
remembered some of it. Now the difficulty
is to give this general idea of main place,
growth, and movement; it is needful to
tack it on a yarn. Now Scotch is the only
History I know; it is the only history
reasonably represented in my library; it is
a very good one for my purpose, owing to
two civilisations having been face to face
throughout — or rather Roman civilisation
face to face with our ancient barbaric life
and government, down to yesterday, to
1750 anyway. But the *Tales of a Grandfather* stand in my way; I am teaching
them to Austin now, and they have all
Scott's defects and all Scott's hopeless
merit. I cannot compete with that; and
yet, so far as regards teaching History,
how he has missed his chances! I think
I 'll try; I really have some historic sense,

I feel that in my bones. Then there's another thing. Scott never knew the Highlands; he was always a Borderer. He has missed that whole, long, strange, pathetic story of our savages, and, besides, his style is not very perspicuous to childhood. Gad, I think I'll have a flutter. Buridan's Ass! Whether to go, what to attack. Must go to other letters; shall add to this, if I have time.

XIII

MY DEAR COLVIN, MY DEAR COLVIN, —
I wonder how often I 'm going to write it.
In spite of the loss of three days, as I have
to tell, and a lot of weeding and cacao
planting, I have finished since the mail
left four chapters, forty-eight pages of my
Samoa history. It is true that the first
three had been a good deal drafted two
years ago, but they had all to be written
and re-written, and the fourth chapter is
all new. Chapter I. Elements of Discord
— Native. II. Elements of Discord —
Foreign. III. The Success of Laupepa.
IV. Brandeis. V. Will probably be called
"The Rise of Mataafa." VI. *Furor Consularis* — a devil of a long chapter. VII
Stuebel the Pacificator. VIII. Government under the Treaty of Berlin. IX.
Practical Suggestions. Say three-sixths of

it are done, maybe more; by this mail five
chapters should go, and that should be a
good half of it; say sixty pages. And if
you consider that I sent by last mail the
end of the *Wrecker*, coming on for seventy
or eighty pages, and the mail before that
the entire Tale of the *Beach of Falsed*, I do
not think I can be accused of idleness.
This is my season; I often work six and
seven, and sometimes eight hours; and the
same day I am perhaps weeding or planting
for an hour or two more — and I dare say
you know what hard work weeding is —
and it all agrees with me at this time of
the year — like — like idleness, if a man of
my years could be idle.

My first visit to Apia was a shock to
me; every second person the ghost of himself, and the place reeking with infection.
But I have not got the thing yet, and hope
to escape. This shows how much stronger
I am; think of me flitting through a town
of influenza patients seemingly unscathed.
We are all on the cacao planting.

The next day my wife and I rode over to the German plantation, Vailele, whose manager is almost the only German left to speak to us. Seventy labourers down with influenza! It is a lovely ride, half-way down our mountain towards Apia, then turn to the right, ford the river, and three miles of solitary grass and cocoa palms, to where the sea beats and the wild wind blows unceasingly about the plantation house. On the way down Fanny said, "Now what would you do if you saw Colvin coming up?"

Next day we rode down to Apia to make calls.

Yesterday the mail came, and the fat was in the fire.

Nov. 29th ?

Book.[1] All right. I must say I like your order. And the papers are some of them up to dick, and no mistake. I agree

---

[1] *Across the Plains.* The papers specially referred to in the next lines are those written at Saranac Lake in the winter of 1887–8, including *A Letter to a Young Gentleman, Pulvis et Umbra, A Christmas Sermon.*

1891
Nov.

with you the lights seem a little turned down. The truth is, I was far through (if you understand Scots), and came none too soon to the South Seas, where I was to recover peace of body and mind. No man but myself knew all my bitterness in those days. Remember that, the next time you think I regret my exile. And however low the lights are, the stuff is true, and I believe the more effective; after all, what I wish to fight is the best fought by a rather cheerless presentation of the truth. The world must return some day to the word duty, and be done with the word reward. There are no rewards, and plenty duties. And the sooner a man sees that and acts upon it like a gentleman or a fine old barbarian, the better for himself.

There is my usual puzzle about publishers. Chatto ought to have it, as he has all the other essays; these all belong to me, and Chatto publishes on terms. Longman has forgotten the terms we are on; let him look up our first correspondence, and he will see I reserved explicitly, as was my habit, the right to republish as I choose. Had the same arrangement with Henley, Magazine of Art, and with Tulloch, Fraser's. — For any necessary note or preface, it would be a real service if you would undertake the duty yourself. I should love a preface by you, as short or as long as you choose, three sentences, thirty pages, the thing I should like is your name. And the excuse of my great distance seems sufficient. I shall return with this the sheets corrected as far as I have them; the rest I will leave, if you will, to you entirely; let it be your book, and disclaim what you dislike in the preface. You can say it was at my eager prayer. I should say I am the less willing to pass Chatto over, because he behaved the other day in a very handsome manner. He asked leave to reprint *Damien;* I gave it to him as a present, explaining I could receive no emolument for a personal attack. And he took out my share of profits, and

sent them in my name to the Leper Fund.
I could not bear after that to take from
him any of that class of books which I
have always given him. Tell him the same
terms will do, Clark to print, uniform with
the others.

I have lost all the days since this letter
began re-handling Chapter IV. of the
Samoa racket. I do not go in for literature; address myself to sensible people
rather than to sensitive. And, indeed, it
is a kind of journalism, I have no right to
dally; if it is to help, it must come soon.
In two months from now it shall be done,
and should be published in the course of
March. I propose Cassell gets it. I am
going to call it "A Footnote to History:
Eight Years of Trouble in Samoa," I
believe. I recoil from serious names;
they seem so much too pretentious for a
pamphlet. It will be about the size of
Treasure Island, I believe. Of course, as
you now know, my case of conscience
cleared itself off, and I began my interven-

tion directly to one of the parties. The other, the Chief Justice, I am to inform of my book the first occasion. God knows if the book will do any good — or harm; but I judge it right to try. There is one man's life certainly involved; and it may be all our lives. I must not stand and slouch, but do my best as best I can. But you may conceive the difficulty of a history extending to the present week, at least, and where almost all the actors upon all sides are of my personal acquaintance. The only way is to judge slowly, and write boldly, and leave the issue to fate. . . . I am far indeed from wishing to confine myself to creative work; that is a loss, the other repairs; the one chance for a man, and, above all, for one who grows elderly, ahem, is to vary drainage and repair. That is the one thing I understand — the cultivation of the shallow *solum* of my brain. But I would rather, from soon on, be released from the obligation to write. In five or six years this plantation —

suppose it and us still to exist — should pretty well support us and pay wages; not before, and already the six years seem long to me. If literature were but a pastime!

I have interrupted myself to write the necessary notification to the Chief Justice.

I see in looking up Longman's letter that it was as usual the letter of an obliging gentleman; so do not trouble him with my reminder. I wish all my publishers were not so nice. And I have a fourth and a fifth baying at my heels; but for these, of course, they must go wanting.

Dec. 2nd.

No answer from the Chief Justice, which is like him, but surely very wrong in such a case. The lunch bell! I have been off work, playing patience and weeding all morning. Yesterday and the day before I drafted eleven and revised nine pages of Chapter V., and the truth is, I was extinct by lunch-time, and played patience sourly the rest of the day. To-morrow or next day I hope to go in again and win. Lunch 2nd Bell.

Dec. 2nd, afternoon.

I have kept up the idleness; blew on the pipe to Belle's piano; then had a ride in the forest all by my nainsel; back and piped again, and now dinner nearing. Take up this sheet with nothing to say. The weird figure of Faauma is in the room washing my windows, in a black lavalava (kilt) with a red handkerchief hanging from round her neck between her breasts; not another stitch; her hair close cropped and oiled; when she first came here she was an angelic little stripling, but she is now in full flower — or half-flower — and grows buxom. As I write, I hear her wet cloth moving and grunting with some industry; for I had a word this day with her husband on the matter of work and meal-time, when she is always late. And she has a vague reverence for Papa, as she and her enormous husband address me when anything

is wrong. Her husband is Lafaele, sometimes called the archangel, of whom I have
writ you often. Rest of our household,
Talolo, cook; Pulu, kitchen boy, good,
steady, industrious lads; Henry, back
again from Savaii, where his love affair
seems not to have prospered, with what
looks like a spear-wound in the back of his
head, of which Mr. Reticence says nothing; Simi, Manuele, and two other labourers
out-doors. Lafaele is provost of the live-
stock, whereof now, three milk-cows, one
bull-calf, one heifer, Jack, Macfarlane, the
mare, Harold, Tifaga Jack, Donald and
Edinburgh — seven horses — O, and the
stallion — eight horses; five cattle; total,
if my arithmetic be correct, thirteen head
of beasts; I don't know how the pigs
stand, or the ducks, or the chickens; but
we get a good many eggs, and now and
again a duckling or a chickling for the
table; the pigs are more solemn, and
appear only on birthdays and sich.

Monday, Dec. 7.

On Friday morning about eleven 1500 cacao seeds arrived, and we set to and toiled from twelve that day to six, and went to bed pretty tired. Next day I got about an hour and a half at my History, and was at it again by 8. 10, and except an hour for lunch kept at it till four P. M. Yesterday, I did some History in the morning, and slept most of the afternoon; and to-day, being still averse from physical labour, and the mail drawing nigh, drew out of the squad, and finished for press the fifth chapter of my History; fifty-nine pages in one month; which (you will allow me to say) is a devil of a large order; it means at least 177 pages of writing; 89,000 words! and hours going to and fro among my notes. However, this is the way it has to be done; the job must be done fast, or it is of no use. And it is a curious yarn. Honestly, I think people should be amused and convinced, if they could be at the pains to look at such a damned outlandish piece of machinery, which of course they won't. And much I care.

When I was filling baskets all Saturday, in my dull mulish way, perhaps the slowest worker there, surely the most particular, and the only one that never looked up or knocked off, I could not but think I should have been sent on exhibition as an example to young literary men. Here is how to learn to write, might be the motto. You should have seen us; the verandah was like an Irish bog; our hands and faces were bedaubed with soil; and Faauma was supposed to have struck the right note when she remarked (*à propos* of nothing), "Too much *eleele* (soil) for me!" The cacao (you must understand) has to be planted at first in baskets of plaited cocoa-leaf. From four to ten natives were plaiting these in the wood-shed. Four boys were digging up soil and bringing it by the boxful to the verandah. Lloyd and I and Belle, and sometimes S. (who came to bear a hand), were filling the baskets, removing stones and lumps of clay; Austin and Faauma carried them when full to Fanny, who planted a seed in each, and then set them, packed close, in the corners of the verandah. From twelve on Friday till five P. M. on Saturday we planted the first 1500, and more than 700 of a second lot. You cannot dream how filthy we were, and we were all properly tired. They are all at ·it again to-day, bar Belle and me, not required, and glad to be out of it. The Chief Justice has not yet replied, and I have news that he received my letter. What a man!

I have gone crazy over Bourget's *Sensations d'Italie;* hence the enclosed dedication,[1] a mere cry of gratitude for the best fun I 've had over a new book this ever so!

[1] For the volume *Across the Plains.*

XIV

Sir,— I have the honour to report further explorations of the course of the river Vaea, with accompanying sketch plan. The party under my command consisted of one horse, and was extremely insubordinate and mutinous, owing to not being used to go into the bush, and being half-broken anyway — and that the wrong half. The route indicated for my party was up the bed of the so-called river Vaea, which I accordingly followed to a distance of perhaps two or three furlongs eastward from the house of Vailima, where the stream being quite dry, the bush thick, and the ground very difficult, I decided to leave the main body of the force under my command tied to a tree, and push on myself with the point of the advance guard, consisting of one man. The valley had

become very narrow and airless; foliage
close shut above; dry bed of the stream
much excavated, so that I passed under
fallen trees without stooping. Suddenly

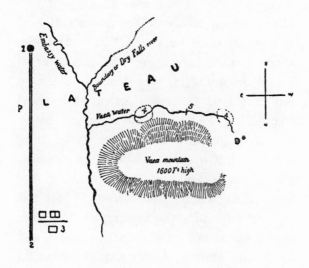

it turned sharply to the north, at right
angles to its former direction; I heard
living water, and came in view of a tall
face of rock and the stream spraying down

it; it might have been climbed, but it would have been dangerous, and I had to make my way up the steep earth banks, where there is nowhere any footing for man, only for trees, which made the rounds of my ladder. I was near the top of this climb, which was very hot and steep, and the pulses were buzzing all over my body, when I made sure there was one external sound in my ears, and paused to listen. No mistake; a sound of a mill-wheel thundering, I thought, close by, yet below me, a huge mill-wheel, yet not going steadily, but with a *schottische* movement, and at each fresh impetus shaking the mountain. There, where I was, I just put down the sound to the mystery of the bush; where no sound now surprises me — and any sound alarms; I only thought it would give Jack a fine fright, down where he stood tied to a tree by himself, and he was badly enough scared when I left him. The good folks at home identified it; it was a sharp earthquake.

At the top of the climb I made my way again to the water-course; it is here running steady and pretty full; strange these intermittencies — and just a little below the main stream is quite dry, and all the original brook has gone down some lava gallery of the mountain — and just a little further below, it begins picking up from the left hand in little boggy tributaries, and in the inside of a hundred yards has grown a brook again.[1] The general course of the

---

[1] As to this peculiar intermittency of the Samoan streams, full in their upper course, but below in many places dry or lost, compare the late Lord Pembroke's *South Sea Bubbles*, p. 212 : — " One odd thing connected with these ravines is the fact that the higher you go the more water you find. Unlike the Thames, which begins, I believe, in half a mile of dusty lane, and expands in its brimming breadth as it approaches the sea, a Samoan stream begins in bubbling plenty and ends in utter drought a mile or two from the salt water. Gradually as you ascend you become more and more hopeful ; moist patches of sand appear here and there, then tiny pools that a fallen leaf might cover, then larger ones with little thread-like runs of water between them : larger and larger, till at last you reach some hard ledge of trap, over which a glorious stream gurgles and splashes into a pool ample enough for the bath of an elephant."

brook was, I guess, S. E. ; the valley still
very deep and whelmed in wood. It
seemed a swindle to have made so sheer a
climb and still find yourself at the bottom
of a well. But gradually the thing seemed
to shallow, the trees to seem poorer and
smaller; I could see more and more of the
silver sprinkles of sky among the foliage,
instead of the sombre piling up of tree
behind tree. And here I had two scares
— first, away up on my right-hand I heard
a bull low; I think it was a bull from the
quality of the low, which was singularly
songful and beautiful; the bulls belong to
me, but how did I know that the bull was
aware of that? and my advance guard not
being at all properly armed, we advanced
with great precaution until I was satisfied
that I was passing eastward of the enemy.
It was during this period that a pool of the
river suddenly boiled up in my face in a
little fountain. It was in a very dreary,
marshy part among dilapidated trees that
you see through holes in the trunks of;

and if any kind of beast or elf or devil had come out of that sudden silver ebullition, I declare I do not think I should have been surprised. It was perhaps a thing as curious — a fish, with which these head waters of the stream are alive. They are some of them as long as my finger, should be easily caught in these shallows, and some day I'll have a dish of them.

Very soon after I came to where the stream collects in another banana swamp, with the bananas bearing well. Beyond, the course is again quite dry; it mounts with a sharp turn a very steep face of the mountain, and then stops abruptly at the lip of a plateau, I suppose the top of Vaea mountain: plainly no more springs here — there was no smallest furrow of a water-course beyond — and my task might be said to be accomplished. But such is the animated spirit in the service that the whole advance guard expressed a sentiment of disappointment that an exploration, so far successfully conducted, should come to a

stop in the most promising view of fresh
successes. And though unprovided either
with compass or cutlass, it was determined
to push some way along the plateau, mark-
ing our direction by the laborious process
of bending down, sitting upon, and thus
breaking the wild cocoanut trees. This was
the less regretted by all from a delightful
discovery made of a huge banyan growing
here in the bush, with flying-buttressed
flying buttresses, and huge arcs of trunk
hanging high overhead and trailing down
new complications of root. I climbed
some way up what seemed the original
beginning; it was easier to climb than a
ship's rigging, even rattled; everywhere
there was foot-hold and hand-hold. It was
judged wise to return and rally the main
body, who had now been left alone for
perhaps forty minutes in the bush.

The return was effected in good order,
but unhappily I only arrived (like so many
other explorers) to find my main body or
rear-guard in a condition of mutiny; the

work, it is to be supposed, of terror. It is
right I should tell you the Vaea has a bad
name, an *aitu fafine* — female devil of
the woods — succubus — haunting it, and
doubtless Jack had heard of her; perhaps,
during my absence, saw her; lucky Jack!
Anyway, he was neither to hold nor to
bind, and finally, after nearly smashing me
by accident, and from mere scare and
insubordination several times, deliberately
set in to kill me; but poor Jack! the tree
he selected for that purpose was a banana!
I jumped off and gave him the heavy end
of my whip over the buttocks! Then I
took and talked in his ear in various
voices; you should have heard my alto — it
was a dreadful, devilish note — I *knew*
Jack *knew* it was an *aitu*. Then I mounted
him again, and he carried me fairly steadily.
He 'll learn yet. He has to learn to trust
absolutely to his rider; till he does, the
risk is always great in thick bush, where a
fellow must try different passages, and put
back and forward, and pick his way by
hair's-breadths.

1891
Dec.
The expedition returned to Vailima in time to receive the visit of the R. C. Bishop. He is a superior man, much above the average of priests.

Thursday.

Yesterday the same expedition set forth to the southward by what is known as Carruthers' Road. At a fallen tree which completely blocks the way, the main body was as before left behind, and the advance guard of one now proceeded with the exploration. At the great tree known as *Mepi Tree*, after Maben the surveyor, the expedition struck forty yards due west till it struck the top of a steep bank which it descended. The whole bottom of the ravine is filled with sharp lava blocks quite unrolled and very difficult and dangerous to walk among; no water in the course, scarce any sign of water. And yet surely water must have made this bold cutting in the plateau. And if so, why is the lava sharp? My science gave out; but

I could not but think it ominous and
volcanic.   The course of the stream was
tortuous, but with a resultant direction a
little by west of north; the sides the whole
way exceeding steep, the expedition buried
under fathoms of foliage.   Presently water
appeared in the bottom, a good quantity;
perhaps thirty or forty cubic feet, with
pools and waterfalls.   A tree that stands
all along the banks here must be very fond
of water; its roots lie close-packed down
the stream, like hanks of guts, so as to
make often a corrugated walk, each root
ending in a blunt tuft of filaments, plainly
to drink water.   Twice there came in small
tributaries from the left or western side —
the whole plateau having a smartish incli-
nation to the east; one of the tributaries
in a handsome little web of silver hanging
in the forest.   Twice I was startled by
birds; one that barked like a dog; another
that whistled loud ploughman's signals, so
that I vow I was thrilled, and thought I had
fallen among runaway blacks, and regretted

my cutlass which I had lost and left behind
while taking bearings. A good many fishes
in the brook, and many cray-fish; one of
the last with a queer glow-worm head.
Like all our brooks, the water is pure as
air, and runs over red stones like rubies.
The foliage along both banks very thick
and high, the place close, the walking
exceedingly laborious. By the time the
expedition reached the fork, it was felt exceedingly questionable whether the *moral*
of the force were sufficiently good to undertake more extended operations. A halt
was called, the men refreshed with water
and a bath, and it was decided at a drum-
head council of war to continue the descent
of the Embassy Water straight for Vailima,
whither the expedition returned, in rather
poor condition, and wet to the waist, about
4 P. M.

Thus in two days the two main water-
courses of this country have been pretty
thoroughly explored, and I conceive my
instructions fully carried out. The main

body of the second expedition was brought
back by another officer despatched for that purpose from Vailima. Casualties: one horse wounded; one man bruised; no deaths — as yet, but the bruised man feels to-day as if his case was mighty serious.

Dec. 25, '91.

Your note with a very despicable bulletin of health arrived only yesterday, the mail being a day behind. It contained also the excellent *Times* article, which was a sight for sore eyes. I am still *taboo;* the blessed Germans will have none of me; and I only hope they may enjoy the *Times* article. 'T is my revenge! I wish you had sent the letter too, as I have no copy, and do not even know what I wrote the last day, with a bad headache, and the mail going out. However, it must have been about right, for the *Times* article was in the spirit I wished to arouse. I hope we can get rid of the man before it is too late. He has set the natives to war; but the natives, by God's blessing, do not want to fight, and I think it will fizzle out — no thanks to the man who tried to start it. But I did not mean to drift into these politics; rather to tell you what I have done since I last wrote.

Well, I worked away at my History for a while, and only got one chapter done; no doubt this spate of work is pretty low now, and will be soon dry; but, God bless you, what a lot I have accomplished; *Wrecker* done, *Beach of Falesá* done, half the *History: c'est étonnant.* (I hear from Burlingame, by the way, that he likes the end of the *Wrecker;* 't is certainly a violent, dark yarn with interesting, plain turns of human nature), then Lloyd and I went down to live in Haggard's rooms, where Fanny presently joined us. Haggard's rooms are in a strange old building — old for Samoa, and has the effect of the antique like some strange monastery; I would tell you more of it, but I think I'm going to use it in a tale. The annexe close by had its door sealed; poor Dowdney lost 1891
Dec. at sea in a schooner. The place is haunted. The vast empty sheds, the empty store, the airless, hot, long, low rooms, the claps of wind that set everything flying — a strange uncanny house to spend Christmas in.

Jan. 1st, '92.

For a day or two I have sat close and 1892
Jan. wrought hard at the *History*, and two more chapters are all but done. About thirty pages should go by this mail, which is not what should be, but all I could overtake. Will any one ever read it? I fancy not; people don't read history for reading, but for education and display — and who desires education in the history of Samoa, with no population, no past, no future, or the exploits of Mataafa, Malietoa, and Consul Knappe? Colkitto and Galasp are a trifle to it. Well, it can't be helped, and it must be done, and better or worse, it's capital fun. There are two to whom I have not been kind — German Consul Becker and English Captain Hand, R. N.

1892
Jan.

On Dec. 30th I rode down with Belle to go to (if you please) the Fancy Ball. When I got to the beach, I found the barometer was below 29°, the wind still in the east and steady, but a huge offensive continent of clouds and vapours forming to leeward. It might be a hurricane; I dared not risk getting caught away from my work, and leaving Belle, returned at once to Vailima. Next day — yesterday — it was a tearer; we had storm shutters up; I sat in my room and wrote by lamplight — ten pages, if you please, seven of them draft, and some of these compiled from as many as seven different and conflicting authorities, so that was a brave day's work. About two a huge tree fell within sixty paces of our house; a little after, a second went; and we sent out boys with axes and cut down a third, which was too near the house, and buckling like a fishing rod. At dinner we had the front door closed and shuttered, the back door open, the lamp lit. The boys in the cook-house were all out at the cook-house door, where we could see them looking in and smiling. Lauilo and Faauma waited on us with smiles. The excitement was delightful. Some very violent squalls came as we sat there, and every one rejoiced; it was impossible to help it; a soul of putty had to sing. All night it blew; the roof was continually sounding under missiles; in the morning the verandahs were half full of branches torn from the forest. There was a last very wild squall about six; the rain, like a thick white smoke, flying past the house in volleys, and as swift, it seemed, as rifle balls; all with a strange, strident hiss, such as I have only heard before at sea, and, indeed, thought to be a marine phenomenon. Since then the wind has been falling with a few squalls, mostly rain. But our road is impassable for horses; we hear a schooner has been wrecked and some native houses blown down in Apia, where Belle is still and must remain a prisoner. Lucky I returned while I could!

But the great good is this; much bread-
fruit and bananas have been destroyed; if
this be general through the islands, famine
will be imminent; and *whoever blows the
coals, there can be no war.* Do I then
prefer a famine to a war? you ask. Not
always, but just now. I am sure the
natives do not want a war; I am sure a
war would benefit no one but the white
officials, and I believe we can easily meet
the famine — or at least that it can be
met. That would give our officials a legi-
timate opportunity to cover their past
errors.

Jan. 2nd.

I woke this morning to find the blow
quite ended. The heaven was all a mottled
gray; even the east quite colourless; the
downward slope of the island veiled in
wafts of vapour, blue like smoke; not a leaf
stirred on the tallest tree; only, three
miles away below me on the barrier reef, I
could see the individual breakers curl and
fall, and hear their conjunct roaring rise,

as it still rises at 1 P. M., like the roar of a
thoroughfare close by.   I did a good morning's work, correcting and clarifying my
draft, and have now finished for press
eight chapters, ninety-one pages, of this
piece of journalism.   Four more chapters,
say fifty pages, remain to be done; I should
gain my wager and finish this volume in
three months, that is to say, the end
should leave me per February mail; I cannot receive it back till the mail of April.
Yes, it can be out in time; pray God that
it be in time to help.

How do journalists fetch up their drivel?
I aim only at clearness and the most obvious
finish, positively at no higher degree of
merit, not even at brevity — I am sure it
could have been all done, with double the
time, in two-thirds of the space.   And yet
it has taken me two months to write
45,500 words; and be damned to my wicked
prowess, I am proud of the exploit!   The
real journalist must be a man not of brass
only, but bronze.   Chapter IX. gapes for

me, but I shrink on the margin, and go on
chattering to you. This last part will be
much less offensive (strange to say) to the
Germans. It is Becker they will never
forgive me for; Knappe I pity and do not
dislike; Becker I scorn and abominate.
Here is the tableau. I. Elements of Discord: Native. II. Elements of Discord:
Foreign. III. The Sorrows of Laupepa.
IV. Brandeis. V. The Battle of Matautu.
VI. Last Exploits of Becker. VII. The
Samoan Camps. VIII. Affairs of Lautii
and Fangalii. IX. *"Furor Consularis."* X.
The Hurricane. XI. Stuebel Recluse. XII.
The Present Government. I estimate the
whole roughly at 70,000 words. Should
anybody ever dream of reading it, it would
be found amusing. $\frac{70000}{300} = 233$ printed
pages; a respectable little five-bob volume,
to bloom unread in shop windows. After
that, I'll have a spank at fiction. And
rest? I shall rest in the grave, or when I
come to Italy. If only the public will
continue to support me! I lost my chance

not dying; there seems blooming little fear 1892 Jan. of it now. I worked close on five hours this morning; the day before, close on nine; and unless I finish myself off with this letter, I'll have another hour and a half, or *aiblins twa*, before dinner. Poor man, how you must envy me, as you hear of these orgies of work, and you scarce able for a letter. But Lord, Colvin, how lucky the situations are not reversed, for I have no situation, nor am fit for any. Life is a steigh brae. Here, have at Knappe, and no more clavers!

3rd.

There was never any man had so many irons in the fire, except Jim Pinkerton.[1] I forgot to mention I have the most gallant suggestion from Lang, with an offer of MS. authorities, which turns my brain. It's all about the throne of Poland and buried treasure in the Mackay country, and Alan Breck can figure there in glory.

[1] In the *Wrecker*. As to the story thus suggested by Mr. Andrew Lang, see below, pp. 245, 246, 272–76.

Yesterday, J. and I set off to Blacklock's (American Consul) who lives not far from that little village I have so often mentioned as lying between us and Apia. I had some questions to ask him for my History; thence we must proceed to Vailele, where I had also to cross-examine the plantation manager about the battle there. We went by a track I had never before followed down the hill to Vaisigano, which flows here in a deep valley, and was unusually full, so that the horses trembled in the ford. The whole bottom of the valley is full of various streams posting between strips of forest with a brave sound of waters. In one place we had a glimpse of a fall some way higher up, and then sparkling in sunlight in the midst of the green valley. Then up by a winding path scarce accessible to a horse for steepness, to the other side, and the open cocoanut glades of the plantation. Here we rode fast, did a mighty satisfactory afternoon's work at the plantation house, and still faster back.

On the return Jack fell with me, but got up again; when I felt him recovering I gave him his head, and he shoved his foot through the rein; I got him by the bit however, and all was well; he had mud over all his face, but his knees were not broken. We were scarce home when the rain began again; that was luck. It is pouring now in torrents; we are in the height of the bad season. Lloyd leaves along with this letter on a change to San Francisco; he had much need of it, but I think this will brace him up. I am, as you see, a tower of strength. I can remember riding not so far and not near so fast when I first came to Samoa, and being shattered next day with fatigue; now I could not tell I have done anything; have re-handled my battle of Fangalii according to yesterday's information — four pages rewritten; and written already some half-dozen pages of letters.

I observe with disgust that while of yore, when I own I was guilty, you never

spared me abuse, but now, when I am so
virtuous, where is the praise? Do admit
that I have become an excellent letter-
writer — at least to you, and that your
ingratitude is imbecile. — Yours ever,
R. L. S.

XV

1892
Jan.

MY DEAR COLVIN, — No letter at all
from you, and this scratch from me! Here
is a year that opens ill. Lloyd is off to
"the coast" sick — *the coast* means Cali-
fornia over most of the Pacific — I have
been down all month with influenza, and
am just recovering — I am overlaid with
proofs, which I am just about half fit to
attend to. One of my horses died this
morning, and another is now dying on the
front lawn — Lloyd's horse and Fanny's.
Such is my quarrel with destiny. But I
am mending famously, come and go on the
balcony, have perfectly good nights, and
though I still cough, have no oppression
and no hemorrhage and no fever. So if I
can find time and courage to add no more,
you will know my news is not altogether

1892
Jan.

of the worst; a year or two ago, and what a state I should have been in now! Your silence, I own, rather alarms me. But I tell myself you have just miscarried; had you been too ill to write, some one would have written me. Understand, I send this brief scratch not because I am unfit to write more, but because I have 58 galleys of the *Wrecker* and 102 of the *Beach of Falesá* to get overhauled somehow or other in time for the mail, and for three weeks I have not touched a pen with my finger.

Feb. 1st.

Feb.

The second horse is still alive, but I still think dying. The first was buried this morning. My proofs are done; it was a rough two days of it, but done. *Consummatum est; na uma.* I believe the *Wrecker* ends well; if I know what a good yarn is, the last four chapters make a good yarn — but pretty horrible. *The Beach of Falesá* I still think well of, but it seems it's immoral and there's a

to-do, and financially it may prove a heavy
disappointment. The plaintive request
sent to me, to make the young folks married properly before "that night," I refused; you will see what would be left
of the yarn, had I consented.[1] This is a
poison bad world for the romancer, this
Anglo-Saxon world; I usually get out of
it by not having any women in it at all;
but when I remember I had the *Treasure
of Franchard* refused as unfit for a family
magazine, I feel despair weigh upon my
wrists.

As I know you are always interested in
novels, I must tell you that a new one is
now entirely planned. It is to be called
Sophia Scarlet, and is in two parts. Part
I. The Vanilla Planter. Part II. The
Overseers. No chapters, I think; just two
dense blocks of narrative, the first of
which is purely sentimental, but the

[1] Editors and publishers had been inclined to shy at
the terms of the fraudulent marriage contract, which is
the pivot of the whole story; see below, Letter XVIII.

second has some rows and quarrels, and winds up with an explosion, if you please! I am just burning to get at Sophia, but I *must* do this Samoan journalism — that 's a cursed duty. The first part of Sophia, bar the first twenty or thirty pages, writes itself; the second is more difficult, involving a good many characters — about ten, I think — who have to be kept all moving, and give the effect of a society. I have three women to handle, out and well-away! but only Sophia is in full tone. Sophia and two men, Windermere, the Vanilla Planter, who dies at the end of Part I., and Rainsforth, who only appears in the beginning of Part II. The fact is, I blush to own it, but Sophia is a *regular novel;* heroine and hero, and false accusation, and love, and marriage, and all the rest of it — all planted in a big South Sea plantation run by ex-English officers — *à la* Stewart's plantation in Tahiti.[1] There is a strong

[1] For a lively account of this plantation and its history, see *South Sea Bubbles,* chap. I.

undercurrent of labour trade, which gives it a kind of Uncle Tom flavour, *absit omen!* The first start is hard; it is hard to avoid a little tedium here, but I think by beginning with the arrival of the three Miss Scarlets hot from school and society in England, I may manage to slide in the information. The problem is exactly a Balzac one, and I wish I had his fist — for I have already a better method — the kinetic, whereas he continually allowed himself to be led into the static. But then he had the fist, and the most I can hope is to get out of it with a modicum of grace and energy, but for sure without the strong impression, the full, dark brush. Three people have had it, the real creator's brush: Scott, see much of *The Antiquary* and *The Heart of Midlothian* (especially all round the trial, before, during, and after) — Balzac — and Thackeray in *Vanity Fair*. Everybody else either paints *thin*, or has to stop to paint, or paints excitedly, so that you see the author skipping before his

canvas.   Here is a long way from poor
Sophia Scarlet!

This day is published

Sophia Scarlet

By

ROBERT LOUIS STEVENSON.

XVI

MY DEAR COLVIN, — This has been a
busyish month for a sick man. First,
Faauma — the bronze candlestick, whom
otherwise I called my butler — bolted from
the bed and bosom of Lafaele, the Archangel Hercules, perfect of the cattle.
There was the deuce to pay, and Hercules
was inconsolable, and immediately started
out after a new wife, and has had one up
on a visit, but says she has "no conversation;" and I think he will take back the
erring and possibly repentent candlestick;
whom we all devoutly prefer, as she is not
only highly decorative, but good-natured,
and if she does little work makes no rows.
I tell this lightly, but it really was a heavy
business; many were accused of complicity,
and Rafael was really very sorry. I had

to hold beds of justice — literally — seated
in my bed and surrounded by lying
Samoans seated on the floor; and there
were many picturesque and still inexpli-
cable . passages. It is hard to reach the
truth in these islands.

The next incident overlapped with this.
S. and Fanny found three strange horses
in the paddock: for long now the boys
have been forbidden to leave their horses
here one hour because our grass is over-
grazed. S. came up with the news, and I
saw I must now strike a blow. "To the
pound with the lot," said I. He proposed
taking the three himself, but I thought
that too dangerous an experiment, said I
should go too, and hurried into my boots
so as to show decision taken, in the necessary interviews. They came of course —
the interviews — and I explained what I
was going to do at huge length, and stuck
to my guns. I am glad to say the natives,
with their usual (purely speculative) sense
of justice highly approved the step after

reflection.   Meanwhile off went S. and I
with the three *corpora delicti;* and a good
job I went!   Once, when our circus began
to kick, we thought all was up; but we got
them down all sound in wind and limb.
I judged I was much fallen off from my
Elliott forefathers, who managed this class
of business with neatness and despatch.
Half-way down it came on to rain tropic
style, and I came back from my outing
drenched like a drowned man — I was
literally blinded as I came back among
these sheets of water; and the consequence
was I was laid down with diarrhœa and
threatenings of Samoa colic for the inside
of another week.

I have a confession to make.   When I
was sick I tried to get to work to finish
that Samoa thing, would n't go; and at
last, in the colic time, I slid off into *David
Balfour,*[1] some 50 pages of which are
drafted, and like me well.   Really I think

---

[1] The sequel to *Kidnapped*, published in the followed
year under the title *Catriona.*

it is spirited; and there's a heroine that
(up to now) seems to have attractions:
absit omen! David, on the whole, seems
excellent. Allan does not come in till the
tenth chapter, and I am only at the eighth,
so I don't know if I can find him again;
but David is on his feet, and doing well,
and very much in love, and mixed up with
the Lord Advocate and the (untitled) Lord
Lovat, and all manner of great folk. And
the tale interferes with my eating and
sleeping. The join is bad; I have not
thought to strain too much for continuity;
so this part be alive, I shall be content.
But there's no doubt David seems to have
changed his style, de'il ha'e him! And
much I care, if the tale travel!

Friday, Feb. ? ? 19th ?

Two incidents to-day which I must
narrate. After lunch, it was raining piti-
lessly; we were sitting in my mother's
bedroom, and I was reading aloud King-
lake's *Charge of the Light Brigade* and we

had just been all seized by the horses
aligning with Lord George Paget, when a
figure appeared on the verandah; a little,
slim, small figure of a lad, with blond (*i. e.*
limed) hair, a propitiatory smile, and a
nose that alone of all his features grew
pale with anxiety. "I come here stop,"
was about the outside of his English; and
I began at once to guess that he was a
runaway labourer,[1] and that the bush-knife
in his hand was stolen. It proved he had
a mate, who had lacked his courage, and
was hidden down the road; they had both
made up their minds to run away, and had
"come here stop." I could not turn out
the poor rogues, one of whom showed me
marks on his back, into the drenching
forest; I could not reason with them, for
they had not enough English, and not one
of our boys spoke their tongue; so I bade
them feed and sleep here to-night, and

---

[1] Most of the work on the plantations in Samoa is
done by "black boys," *i. e.* imported labourers from other
(Melanesian) islands.

to-morrow I must do what the Lord shall bid me.

Near dinner time, I was told that a friend of Lafaele's had found human remains in my bush. After dinner, a figure was seen skulking across towards the waterfall, which produced from the verandah a shout, in my most stentorian tones: "*O ai le ingoa?*" literally "Who the name?" which serves here for "What's your business?" as well. It proved to be Lafaele's friend; I bade a kitchen boy, Lauilo, go with him to see the spot, for though it had ceased raining, the whole island ran and dripped. Lauilo was willing enough, but the friend of the archangel demurred; he had too much business; he had no time. "All right," I said, "you too much frightened, I go along," which of course produced the usual shout of delight from all those who did not require to go. I got into my Saranac snow boots; Lauilo got a cutlass; Mary Carter, our Sydney maid, joined the party for a lark, and off we set.

I tell you our guide kept us moving; for ₁₈₉₂
the dusk fell swift.   Our woods have an _{Feb.}
infamous reputation at the best, and our
errand (to say the least of it) was grisly.
At last they found the remains; they were
old, which was all I cared to be sure of;
it seemed a strangely small "pickle-banes"
to stand for a big, flourishing, buck-
islander, and their situation in the darken-
ing and dripping bush was melancholy.
All at once, I found there was a second
skull, with a bullet-hole I could have stuck
my two thumbs in — say anybody else's
one thumb.   My Samoans said it could not
be, there were not enough bones; I put
the two pieces of skull together, and at
last convinced them.   Whereupon, in a
flash, they found the not unromantic explanation.   This poor brave had succeeded in
the height of a Samoan warrior's ambition;
he had taken a head, which he was never
destined to show to his applauding camp.
Wounded himself, he had crept here into
the bush to die with his useless trophy by

his side. His date would be about fifteen
years ago, in the great battle between
Laupepa and Talavou, which took place on
My Land, Sir. To-morrow we shall bury
the bones and fire a salute in honour of
unfortunate courage.

Do you think I have an empty life? or
that a man jogging to his club has so much
to interest and amuse him? — touch and
try him too, but that goes along with the
others; no pain, no pleasure, is the iron
law. So here I stop again, and leave, as
I left yesterday, my political business
untouched. And lo! here comes my pupil,
I believe, so I stop in time.

March 2nd.

Mar. Since I last wrote, fifteen chapters of
David Balfour have been drafted, and five
tirés au clair. I think it pretty good;
there's a blooming maiden that costs
anxiety — she is as virginal as billy; but
David seems there and alive, and the Lord
Advocate is good, and so I think is an

episodic appearance of the Master of
Lovat. In Chapter xvii. I shall get David
abroad — Alan went already in Chapter
xii. The book should be about the length
of *Kidnapped;* this early part of it, about
D.'s evidence in the Appin case, is more
of a story than anything in *Kidnapped,* but
there is no doubt there comes a break in
the middle, and the tale is practically in
two divisions. In the first James More
and the M'Gregors, and Catriona, only
show; in the second, the Appin case being
disposed of, and James Stewart hung, they
rule the roast and usurp the interest —
should there be any left. Why did I take
up *David Balfour?* I don't know. A
sudden passion.

Monday, I went down in the rain with a
colic to take the chair at a public meeting;
dined with Haggard; sailed off to my
meeting, and fought with wild beasts for
three anxious hours. All was lost that
any sensible man cared for, but the meeting did not break up — thanks a good deal

to R. L. S. — and the man who opposed
my election, and with whom I was all the
time wrangling, proposed the vote of thanks
to me with a certain handsomeness; I
assure you I had earned it. . . . Haggard
and the great Abdul, his high-caste Indian
servant, imported by my wife, were sitting
up for me with supper, and I suppose it
was twelve before I got to bed. Tuesday
raining, my mother rode down, and we
went to the Consulate to sign a Factory
and Commission. Thence, I to the lawyers,
to the printing office, and to the Mission.
It was dinner time when I returned home.

This morning, our cook-boy having suddenly left — injured feelings — the archangel was to cook breakfast. I found him
lighting the fire before dawn; his eyes
blazed, he had no word of any language
left to use, and I saw in him (to my
wonder) the strongest workings of gratified
ambition. Napoleon was no more pleased
to sign his first treaty with Austria than
was Lafaele to cook that breakfast. All

morning, when I had hoped to be at this 1892 Mar. letter, I slept like one drugged, and you must take this (which is all I can give you) for what it is worth —

D. B.

Memoirs of his Adventures at Home and Abroad. The Second Part; wherein are set forth the misfortunes in which he was involved upon the Appin Murder; his troubles with Lord Advocate Prestongrange; captivity on the Bass Rock; journey into France and Holland; and singular relations with James More Drummond or Macgregor, a son of the notorious Rob Roy.

Chapters I. A Beggar on Horseback. II. The Highland Writer. III. I go to Pilrig. IV. Lord Advocate Prestongrange. V. Butter and Thunder. VI. I make a fault in honour. VII. The Bravo. VIII. The Heather on Fire. IX. I begin to be haunted with a red-headed man. X. The Wood by Silvermills. XI. On the march again with Alan. XII. Gillane Sands.

1892
Mar. XIII. The Bass Rock.   XIV. Black Andie's
Tale of Tod Lapraik.   XV. I go to Inverary.

That is it, as far as drafted.   Chapters
IV. V. VII. IX. and XIV. I am specially
pleased with; the last being an episodical
bogie story about the Bass Rock told there
by the Keeper.

XVII

March 9th.

My DEAR S. C., — Take it not amiss if
this is a wretched letter. I am eaten up
with business. Every day this week I
have had some business impediment — I
am even now waiting a deputation of chiefs
about the road — and my precious morning
was shattered by a polite old scourge of a
faipule — parliament man — come begging.
All the time *David Balfour* is skelping
along. I began it the 13th of last month;
I have now 12 chapters, 79 pages ready for
press, or within an ace, and by the time
the month is out, one-half should be completed, and I'll be back at drafting the
second half. What makes me sick is to
think of Scott turning out *Guy Mannering*
in three weeks! What a pull of work:
heavens, what thews and sinews! And

here am I, my head spinning from having
only re-written seven not very difficult
pages — and not very good when done.
Weakling generation. It makes me sick
of myself, to make such a fash and bobbery
over a rotten end of an old nursery yarn,
not worth spitting on when done. Still,
there is no doubt I turn out my work more
easily than of yore; and I suppose I should
be singly glad of that. And if I got my
book done in six weeks, seeing it will be
about half as long as a Scott, and I have to
write everything twice, it would be about
the same rate of industry. It is my fair
intention to be done with it in three
months, which would make me about one-
half the man Sir Walter was for application
and driving the dull pen. Of the merit
we shall not talk; but I don't think Davie
is *without* merit.

March 12th.

And I have this day triumphantly finished
15 chapters, 100 pages — being exactly
one-half (as near as anybody can guess) of

David Balfour; the book to be about a
fifth as long again (altogether) as *Treasure
Island :* could I but do the second half in
another month! But I can't, I fear; I
shall have some belated material arriving
by next mail, and must go again at the
History. Is it not characteristic of my
broken tenacity of mind, that I should
have left Davie Balfour some five years in
the British Linen Company's Office, and
then follow him at last with such vivacity?
But I leave you again; the last (15th)
chapter ought to be re-wrote, or part of it,
and I want the half completed in the
month, and the month is out by midnight;
though, to be sure, last month was February,
and I might take grace. These notes are
only to show I hold you in mind, though I
know they can have no interest for man or
God or animal.

I should have told you about the Club.
We have been asked to try and start a sort
of weekly ball for the half-castes and
natives, ourselves to be the only whites;

and we consented, from a very heavy sense
of duty, and with not much hope. Two
nights ago we had twenty people up,
received them in the front verandah, entertained them on cake and lemonade, and I
made a speech — embodying our proposals,
or conditions, if you like — for I suppose
thirty minutes. No joke to speak to such
an audience, but it is believed I was
thoroughly intelligible. I took the plan
of saying everything at least twice in a
different form of words, so that if the one
escaped my hearers, the other might be
seized. One white man came with his
wife, and was kept rigorously on the front
verandah below! You see what a sea of
troubles this is like to prove; but it is the
only chance — and when it blows up, it
must blow up! I have no more hope in
anything than a dead frog; I go into everything with a composed despair, and don't
mind — just as I always go to sea with the
conviction I am to be drowned, and like it
before all other pleasures. But you should

have seen the return voyage, when nineteen horses had to be found in the dark,
and nineteen bridles, all in a drench of
rain, and the club, just constituted as such,
sailed away in the wet, under a cloudy
moon like a bad shilling, and to descend a
road through the forest that was at that
moment the image of a respectable mountain brook. My wife, who is president
with power to expel, had to begin her
functions. . . .

25th March

Heaven knows what day it is, but I am
ashamed, all the more as your letter from
Bournemouth of all places — poor old
Bournemouth! — is to hand, and contains
a statement of pleasure in my letters which
I wish I could have rewarded with a long
one. What has gone on? A vast of
affairs, of a mingled, strenuous, incon-
clusive, desultory character; much waste
of time, much riding to and fro, and little
transacted or at least peracted.

Let me give you a review of the present

state of our live stock. — Six boys in the bush; six souls about the house. Talolo, the cook, returns again to-day, after an absence which has cost me about twelve hours of riding, and I suppose eight hours' solemn sitting in council. "I am sorry indeed for the Chief Justice of Samoa," I said; "it is more than I am fit for to be Chief Justice of Vailima." — Lauilo is steward. Both these are excellent servants; we gave a luncheon party when we buried the Samoan bones, and I assure you all was in good style, yet we never interfered. The food was good, the wine and dishes went round as by mechanism. — Steward's assistant and washman. Arrick, a New Hebridee black boy, hired from the German firm; not so ugly as most, but not pretty neither; not so dull as his sort are, but not quite a Crichton. When he came first, he ate so much of our good food that he got a prominent belly. Kitchen assistant, Tomas (Thomas in English), a Fiji man, very tall and handsome, moving like

a marionette with sudden bounds, and rolling his eyes with sudden effort. — Washer-
woman and precentor, Helen, Tomas's
wife. This is our weak point; we are
ashamed of Helen; the cook-house blushes
for her; they murmur there at her presence.
She seems all right; she is not a bad-
looking, strapping wench, seems chaste, is
industrious, has an excellent taste in hymns
— you should have heard her read one
aloud the other day, she marked the
rhythm with so much gloating, dissenter
sentiment. What is wrong, then? says
you. Low in your ear — and don't let the
papers get hold of it — she is of no family.
None, they say; literally a common woman.
Of course, we have out-islanders, who *may*
be villeins; but we give them the benefit
of the doubt, which is impossible with
Helen of Vailima; our blot, out pitted
speck. The pitted speck I have said is
our precentor. It is always a woman who
starts Samoan song; the men who sing
second do not enter for a bar or two.

Poor, dear Faauma, the unchaste, the extruded Eve of our Paradise, knew only two hymns; but Helen seems to know the whole repertory, and the morning prayers go far more lively in consequence. — Lafaele, provost of the cattle. The cattle are Jack, my horse, quite converted, my wife rides him now, and he is as steady as a doctor's cob; Tifaga Jack, a circus horse, my mother's piebald, bought from a passing circus; Belle's mare, now in childbed or next door, confound the slut! Musu — amusingly translated the other day "don't want to," literally cross, but always in the sense of stubbornness and resistance — my wife's little dark-brown mare, with a white star on her forehead, whom I have been riding of late to steady her — she has no vices, but is unused, skittish and uneasy, and wants a lot of attention and humouring; lastly (of saddle horses) Luna — not the Latin *moon*, the Hawaiian *overseer*, but it's pronounced the same — a pretty little mare too, but scarce at all broken, a bad bucker, and has to be ridden with a stock-whip and be brought back with her rump criss-crossed like a clan tartan; the two cart horses, now only used with pack-saddles; two cows, one in the straw (I trust) to-morrow, a third cow, the Jersey — whose milk and temper are alike subjects of admiration — she gives good exercise to the farming saunterer, and refreshes him on his return with cream; two calves, a bull, and a cow; God knows how many ducks and chickens, and for a wager not even God knows how many cats; twelve horses, seven horses, five kine: is not this Babylon the Great which I have builded? Call it *Subpriorsford.*

Two nights ago the club had its first meeting; only twelve were present, but it went very well. I was not there, I had ridden down the night before after dinner on my endless business, took a cup of tea in the Mission like an ass, then took a cup of coffee like a fool at Haggard's, then fell into a discussion with the American

Consul . . . I went to bed at Haggard's,
came suddenly broad awake, and lay sleepless the live night. It fell chill, I had
only a sheet, and had to make a light and
range the house for a cover — I found one in
the hall, a mackintosh. So back to my
sleepless bed, and to lie there till dawn.
In the morning I had a longish ride to take
in a day of a blinding, staggering sun, and
got home by eleven, our luncheon hour,
with my head rather swimmy; the only
time I have *feared* the sun since I was in
Samoa. However, I got no harm, but did
not go to the club, lay off, lazied, played
the pipe, and read a novel by James Payn
— sometimes quite interesting, and in one
place really very funny with the quaint
humour of the man. Much interested the
other day. As I rode past a house, I saw
where a Samoan had written a word on
a board, and there was an Ⅴ, perfectly
formed, but upside down. You never saw
such a thing in Europe; but it is as
common as dirt in Polynesia. Men's

names are tattooed on the forearm; it is common to find a subverted letter tattooed there. Here is a tempting problem for psychologists.

I am now on terms again with the German Consulate, I know not for how long; not, of course, with the President, which I find a relief; still, with the Chief Justice and the English Consul. For Haggard, I have a genuine affection; he is a lovable man.

Wearyful man! "Here is the yarn of Loudon Dodd, *not as he told it, but as it was afterwards written.*"[1] These word were left out by some carelessness, and I think I have been thrice tackled about them. Grave them in your mind and wear them on your forehead.

The Lang story will have very little about the treasure; *The Master*[2] will

[1] In answer to the obvious remark that the length and style of the *Wrecker*, then running in Scribner's Magazine, were out of keeping with what professed at the outset to be a spoken yarn.

[2] *Of Ballantrae.*

appear; and it is to a great extent a tale of
Prince Charlie *after* the '45, and a love
story forbye: the hero is a melancholy
exile, and marries a young woman who
interests the prince, and there is the devil
to pay. I think the Master kills him in a
duel, but don't know yet, not having yet
seen my second heroine. No — the Master
does n't kill him, they fight, he is wounded,
and the Master plays *deus ex machina.* *I
think* just now of calling it *The Tail of the
Race;* no — heavens! I never saw till this
moment — but of course nobody but myself
would ever understand Mill-Race, they
would think of a quarter-mile. So — I am
nameless again. My melancholy young
man is to be quite a Romeo. Yes, I 'll
name the book from him: *Dyce of Ythan*
— pronounce Eethan.

Dyce of Ythan
by R. L. S.

Oh, Shovel — Shovel waits his turn, he
and his ancestors. I would have tackled
him before, but my *State Trials* have

never come. So that I have now quite
planned : —

Dyce of Ythan. (Historical, 1750.)

Sophia Scarlet. (To-day.)

The Shovels of Newton French. (Historical, 1650 to 1830.)

And quite planned and part written : —

The Pearl Fisher. (To-day.) (With Lloyd, a machine.)[1]

David Balfour. (Historical, 1751.)

And, by a strange exception for R. L. S., all in the third person except D. B.

I don't know what day this is now (the 29th), but I have finished my two chapters, ninth and tenth, of *Samoa* in time for the mail, and feel almost at peace. The tenth was the hurricane, a difficult problem; it so tempted one to be literary; and I feel sure the less of that there is in my little handbook, the more chance it has of some utility. Then the events are complicated, seven ships to tell of, and sometimes three of them together; Oh, it was quite a

---

[1] Afterwards changed into *The Ebb Tide.*

job. But I think I have my facts pretty correct, and for once, in my sickening yarn, they are handsome facts: creditable to all concerned; not to be written of — and I should think, scarce to be read — without a thrill. I doubt I have got no hurricane into it, the intricacies of the yarn absorbing me too much. But there — it 's done somehow, and time presses hard on my heels. The book, with my best expedition, may come just too late to be of use. In which case I shall have made a handsome present of some months of my life for nothing and to nobody. Well, through Her the most ancient heavens are fresh and strong.[1]

30th.

After I had written you, I re-read my hurricane, which is very poor; the life of the journalist is hard, another couple of writings and I could make a good thing, I believe, and it must go as it is! But, of course, this book is not written for honour

---

[1] Wordsworth, a shade misquoted.

and glory, and the few who will read it may not know the difference. Very little time. I go down with the mail shortly, dine at the Chinese restaurant, and go to the club to dance with islandresses. Think of my going out once a week to dance.

Politics are on the full job again, and we don't know what is to come next. I think the whole treaty *raj* seems quite played out! They have taken to bribing the *faipule* men (parliament men) to stay in Mulinuu, we hear; but I have not yet sifted the rumour. I must say I shall be scarce surprised if it prove true; these rumours have the knack of being right.— Our weather this last month has been tremendously hot, not by the thermometer, which sticks at 86°, but to the sensation: no rain, no wind, and this the storm month. It looks ominous, and is certainly disagreeable.

No time to finish,

Yours ever,

R. L. S.

XVIII

1892
May.

MY DEAR COLVIN, — As I rode down last night about six, I saw a sight I must try to tell you of. In front of me, right over the top of the forest into which I was descending was a vast cloud. The front of it accurately represented the somewhat rugged, long-nosed, and beetle-browed profile of a man, crowned by a huge Kalmuck cap; the flesh part was of a heavenly pink, the cap, the moustache, the eyebrows were of a bluish gray; to see this with its childish exactitude of design and colour, and hugeness of scale — it covered at least 25° — held me spellbound. As I continued to gaze, the expression began to change; he had the exact air of closing one eye, dropping his jaw, and drawing down his nose; had the thing not been so imposing,

I could have smiled; and then almost in a moment, a shoulder of leaden-coloured bank drove in front and blotted it. My attention spread to the rest of the cloud, and it was a thing to worship. It rose from the horizon, and its top was within thirty degrees of the zenith; the lower parts were like a glacier in shadow, varying from dark indigo to a clouded white in exquisite gradations. The sky behind, so far as I could see, was all of a blue already enriched and darkened by the night, for the hill had what lingered of the sunset. But the top of my Titanic cloud flamed in broad sunlight, with the most excellent softness and brightness of fire and jewels, enlightening all the world. It must have been far higher than Mount Everest, and its glory, as I gazed up at it out of the night, was beyond wonder. Close by rode the little crescent moon; and right over its western horn, a great planet of about equal lustre with itself. The dark woods below were shrill with that noisy business of the birds'

evening worship. When I returned, after
eight, the moon was near down; she
seemed little brighter than before, but now
that the cloud no longer played its part of
a nocturnal sun, we could see that sight,
so rare with us at home that it was counted
a portent, so customary in the tropics, of
the dark sphere with its little gilt band
upon the belly. The planet had been
setting faster, and was now below the
crescent. They were still of an equal
brightness.

I could not resist trying to reproduce
this in words, as a specimen of these
incredibly beautiful and imposing meteors
of the tropic sky that make so much of my
pleasure here; though a ship's deck is
the place to enjoy them. Oh, what *awful*
scenery, from a ship's deck, in the tropics!
People talk about the Alps, but the clouds
of the trade wind are alone for sublimity.

Now to try and tell you what has been
happening. The state of these islands,
and of Mataafa and Laupepa (Malietoa's

ambo) had been much on my mind.   I went
to the priests and sent a message to
Mataafa, at a time when it was supposed
he was about to act.   He did not act,
delaying in true native style, and I determined I should go to visit him.   I have
been very good not to go sooner; to live
within a few miles of a rebel camp, to be a
novelist, to have all my family forcing me
to go, and to refrain all these months,
counts for virtue.   But hearing that several
people had gone and the government done
nothing to punish them, and having an
errand there which was enough to justify
myself in my own eyes, I half determined
to go, and spoke of it with the half-caste
priest.   And here (confound it) up came
Laupepa and his guards to call on me; we
kept him to lunch, and the old gentleman
was very good and amiable.   He asked me
why I had not been to see him?   I reminded
him a law had been made, and told him I
was not a small boy to go and ask leave of
the consuls, and perhaps be refused.   He

told me to pay no attention to the law but
come when I would, and begged me to
name a day to lunch. The next day (I
think it was) early in the morning, a man
appeared; he had metal buttons like a
policeman — but he was none of our Apia
force; he was a rebel policeman, and had
been all night coming round inland through
the forest from Malie.   He brought a letter
addressed

> *I laua susuga*   To his Excellency
> *Misi Mea.*   Mr. Thingumbob.

(So as not to compromise me.)   I can read
Samoan now, though not speak it.   It was
to ask me for last Wednesday.   My difficulty was great; I had no man here who
was fit, or who would have cared, to write
for me; and I had to postpone the visit.
So I gave up half-a-day with a groan, went
down to the priests, arranged for Monday
week to go to Malie, and named Thursday
as my day to lunch with Laupepa.   I was
sharply ill on Wednesday, mail day.   But
on Thursday I had to trail down and go

through the dreary business of a feast, in the King's wretched shanty, full in view of the President's fine new house; it made my heart burn.

This gave me my chance to arrange a private interview with the King, and I decided to ask Mr. Whitmee, one of our missionaries, to be my interpreter. On Friday, being too much exhausted to go down, I begged him to come up. He did, I told him the heads of what I meant to say; and he not only consented, but said, if we got on well with the King, he would even proceed with me to Malie. Yesterday, in consequence, I rode down to W.'s house by eight in the morning; waited till ten; received a message that the King was stopped by a meeting with the President and *faipule;* made another engagement for seven at night; came up; went down; waited till eight, and came away again, *bredouille,* and a dead body. The poor, weak, enslaved King had not dared to come to me even in secret. Now I have

to-day for a rest, and to-morrow to Malie.
Shall I be suffered to embark? It is
very doutbful; they are on the trail. On
Thursday, a policeman came up to me and
began that a boy had been to see him, and
said I was going to see Mataafa. — "And
what did you say?" said I. — "I told him
I did not know about where you were
going," said he. — "A very good answer,"
said I, and turned away. It is lashing rain
to-day, but to-morrow, rain or shine, I
must at least make the attempt; and I am
so weary, and the weather looks so bad. I
could half wish they would arrest me on
the beach. All this bother and pother to
try and bring a little chance of peace; all
this opposition and obstinacy in people
who remain here by the mere forbearance
of Mataafa, who has a great force within
six miles of their government buildings,
which are indeed only the residences of
white officials. To understand how I have
been occupied, you must know that "Misi
Mea" has had another letter, and this time

had to answer himself; think of doing so
in a language so obscure to me, with the
aid of a Bible, concordance and dictionary!
What a wonderful Baboo compilation it
must have been! I positively expected to
hear news of its arrival in Malie by the
sound of laughter. I doubt if you will be
able to read this scrawl, but I have managed
to scramble somehow up to date; and.to-
morrow, one way or another, should be
interesting. But as for me, I am a wreck,
as I have no doubt style and handwriting
both testify.

8 P. M.

Wonderfully rested; feel almost fit for
to-morrow's deary excursion — not that it
will be dreary if the weather favour, but
otherwise it will be death; and a native
feast, and I fear I am in for a big one, is a
thing I loathe. I wonder if you can really
conceive me as a politician in this extra-
mundane sphere — presiding at public
meetings, drafting proclamations, receiv-
ing mis-addressed letters that have been

carried all night through tropical forests?
It seems strange indeed, and to you who
know me really, must seem stranger. I
do not say I am free from the itch of meddling, but God knows this is no tempting
job to meddle in; I smile at picturesque
circumstances like the Misi Mea (*Monsieur
Chose* is the exact equivalent) correspondence, but the business as a whole bores
and revolts me. I do nothing and say
nothing; and then a day comes, and I say
"this can go on no longer."

9.30 P. M.

The wretched native dilatoriness finds
me out. News has just come that we must
embark at six to-morrow; I have divided
the night in watches, and hope to be called
to-morrow at four and get under way by
five. It is a great chance if it be managed;
but I have given directions and lent my
own clock to the boys, and hope the best.
If I get called at four we shall do it nicely.
Good-night; I must turn in.

May 3rd.

Well, we did get off by about 5.30, or, by'r lady! quarter of six: myself on Donald, the huge gray cart-horse, with a ship-bag across my saddle bow, Fanny on Musu and Belle on Jack. We were all feeling pretty tired and sick, and I looked like heaven knows what on the cart horse: "death on the pale horse," I suggested — and young Hunt the missionary, who met me to-day on the same charger, squinted up at my perch and remarked, "There's a sweet little cherub that sits up aloft." The boat was ready and we set off down the lagoon about seven, four oars, and Talolo, my cook, steering.

May 9th, (Monday anyway).

And see what good resolutions came to! Here is all this time past, and no speed made. Well, we got to Malie and were received with the most friendly consideration by the rebel chief. Belle and Fanny were obviously thought to be my two wives; they were served their kava to-

gether, as were Mataafa and myself. Talolo
utterly broke down as interpreter; long
speeches were made to me by Mataafa and
his orators, of which he could make nothing but they were "very much surprised"
— his way of pronouncing obliged — and
as he could understand nothing that fell
from me except the same form of words,
the dialogue languished and all business
had to be laid aside.   We had kava,[1] and

[1] "Kava, properly Ava, is a drink more or less intoxi-
cating, made from the root of the *Piper Methysticum*, a
Pepper plant.   The root is grated : formerly it was chewed
by fair damsels.   The root thus broken up is rubbed about
in a great pail, with water slowly added.   A strainer of
bark cloth is plunged into it at times, and wrung out so as
to carry away the small fragments of root.   The drink is
made and used in ceremony.   Every detail is regulated by
rules, and the manner of the mixture of the water, the
straining, the handling of the cup, the drinking out of it
and returning, should all be done according to a well-
established manner and in certain cadences."   I have ven-
tured to borrow this explanation from Mr. Lafarge's notes
to his catalogue of South Sea Drawings.   It may serve to
make clearer several passages in later letters of the present
collection (*e. g.* pp. 195, 210, 315).   Readers of the late
Lord Pembroke's *South Sea Bubbles* will remember the
account of this beverage and its preparation in chap. VIII.
of that volume.

then a dish of arrowroot; one end of the house was screened off for us with a fine tapa, and we lay and slept, the three of us, heads and tails, upon the mats till dinner. After dinner his illegitimate majesty and myself had a walk, and talked as well as my twopenny Samoan would admit. Then there was a dance to amuse the ladies before the house, and we came back by moonlight, the sky piled full of high faint clouds that long preserved some of the radiance of the sunset. The lagoon was very shallow; we continually struck, for the moon was young and the light baffling; and for a long time we were accompanied by, and passed and re-passed, a huge whale-boat from Savaii, pulling perhaps twelve oars, and containing perhaps forty people who sang in time as they went. So to the hotel, where we slept, and returned the next Tuesday morning on the three same steeds.

Meanwhile my business was still un-transacted. And on Saturday morning, I

sent down and arranged with Charlie
Taylor to go down that afternoon. I had
scarce got the saddle bags fixed and had
not yet mounted, when the rain began.
But it was no use delaying now; off I
went in a wild waterspout to Apia; found
Charlie (Salé) Taylor — a sesquipedalian
young half-caste — not yet ready, had a
snack of bread and cheese at the hotel
while waiting him, and then off to Malie.
It rained all the way, seven miles; the
road, which begins in triumph, dwindles
down to a nasty, boggy, rocky footpath
with weeds up to a horseman's knees; and
there are eight pig fences to jump, nasty
beastly jumps — the next morning we found
one all messed with blood where a horse
had come to grief — but my Jack is a clever
fencer; and altogether we made good time,
and got to Malie about dark. It is a
village of very fine native houses, high,
domed, oval buildings, open at the sides,
or only closed with slatted Venetians. To
be sure, Mataafa's is not the worst. It

was already quite dark within, only a little
fire of cocoa-shell blazed in the midst and
showed us four servants; the chief was in
his chapel, whence we heard the sound of
chaunting. Presently he returned; Taylor
and I had our soaking clothes changed,
family worship was held, kava brewed, I
was exhibited to the chiefs as a man who
had ridden through all that rain and risked
deportation to serve their master; they
were bidden learn my face, and remember
upon all occasions to help and serve me.
Then dinner, and politics, and fine speeches
until twelve at night — Oh, and some more
kava — when I could sit up no longer; my
usual bed-time is eight, you must remember. Then one end of the house was
screened off for me alone, and a bed made
— you never saw such a couch — I believe
of nearly fifty (half at least) fine mats, by
Mataafa's daughter, Kalala. Here I re-
posed alone; and on the other side of the
tafa, Majesty and his household. Armed
guards and a drummer patrolled about the

house all night; they had no shift, poor
devils; but stood to arms from sun-down
to sun-up.

About four in the morning, I was awakened by the sound of a whistle pipe blown
outside on the dark, very softly and to a
pleasing simple air; I really think I have
hit the first phrase:

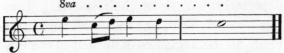

It sounded very peaceful, sweet and strange
in the dark; and I found this was a part of
the routine of my rebel's night, and it was
done (he said) to give good dreams. By a
little before six, Taylor and I were in the
saddle again fasting. My riding boots
were so wet I could not get them on, so I
must ride barefoot. The morning was fair
but the roads very muddy, the weeds soaked
us nearly to the waist, Salé was twice spilt
at the fences, and we got to Apia a be-
draggled enough pair. All the way along

the coast, the paté (small wooden drum) was
beating in the villages and the people
crowding to the churches in their fine
clothes. Thence through the mangrove
swamp, among the black mud and the
green mangroves, and the black and scarlet
crabs, to Mulinuu, to the doctor's, where
I had an errand, and so to the inn to breakfast about nine. After breakfast I rode
home. Conceive such an outing, remember the pallid brute that lived in Skerryvore
like a weevil in a biscuit, and receive the
intelligence that I was rather the better
for my journey. Twenty miles ride, sixteen fences taken, ten of the miles in a
drenching rain, seven of them fasting and
in the morning chill, and six stricken
hours' political discussions by an interpreter; to say nothing of sleeping in
a native house, at which many of our
excellent literati would look askance of
itself.

You are to understand: if I take all this
bother, it is not only from a sense of duty,

1892
May

or a love of meddling — damn the phrase,
take your choice — but from a great affection for Mataafa. He is a beautiful, sweet
old fellow, and he and I grew quite fulsome on Saturday night about our senti-
ments. I had a messenger from him to-day
with a flannel undershirt which I had left
behind like a gibbering idiot; and per-
petrated in reply another baboo letter. It
rains again to-day without mercy; blessed,
welcome rains, making up for the paucity
of the late wet season; and when the
showers slacken, I can hear my stream
roaring in the hollow, and tell myself that
the cacaos are drinking deep. I am desperately hunted to finish my Samoa book
before the mail goes; this last chapter is
equally delicate and necessary. The
prayers of the congregation are requested.
Eheu! and it will be ended before this
letter leaves and printed in the States
ere you can read this scribble. The first
dinner gong has sounded; *je vous salue,
monsieur et cher confrère. Tofa, soifua!*

Sleep! long life! as our Samoan salutation
of farewell runs.

Friday, May 13th.

Well; the last chapter, by far the most difficult and ungrateful, is well under way, I have been from six to seven hours upon it daily since I last wrote; and that is all I have done forbye working at Samoan rather hard, and going down on Wednesday evening to the club. I make some progress now at the language; I am teaching Belle, which clears and exercises myself. I am particularly taken with the *finesse* of the pronouns. The pronouns are all dual and plural and the first person, both in the dual and plural, has a special exclusive and inclusive form. You can conceive what fine effects of precision and distinction can be reached in certain cases. Take Ruth, i, *vv.* 8 to 13, and imagine how those pronouns come in; it is exquisitely elegant, and makes the mouth of the *littérateur* to water. I am going to exercitate my pupil over those verses to-day for pronoun practice.

Tuesday.

1892
May   Yesterday came yours. Well, well, if
the dears prefer a week, why, I 'll give
them ten days, but the real document,
from which I have scarcely varied, ran for
one night.[1] I think you seem scarcely
fair to Wiltshire, who had surely, under
his beast-ignorant ways, right noble quali-
ties. And I think perhaps you scarce do
justice to the fact that this is a place of
realism *à outrance;* nothing extenuated or
coloured. Looked at so, is it not, with all
its tragic features, wonderfully idyllic,
with great beauty of scene and circum-
stance? And will you please to observe
that almost all that is ugly is in the
whites? I 'll apologize for Papa Randal if
you like; but if I told you the whole truth
— for I did extenuate there! — and he
seemed to me essential as a figure, and
essential as a pawn in the game, Wiltshire's
disgust for him being one of the small,

---

[1] Referring to the marriage contract in the *Beach of
Falesá :* see above, Letter xv.

efficient motives in the story. Now it would have taken a fairish dose to disgust Wiltshire. — Again, the idea of publishing the Beach substantively is dropped — at once, both on account of expostulation, and because it measured shorter than I had expected. And it was only taken up, when the proposed volume, *Beach de Mar*, petered out. It petered out thus : the chief of the short stories got sucked into *Sophia Scarlet* — and Sophia is a book I am much taken with, and mean to get to, as soon as — but not before — I have done *David Balfour* and *The Young Chevalier.* So you see you are like to hear no more of the Pacific or the nineteenth century for a while. *The Young Chevalier* is a story of sentiment and passion, which I mean to write a little differently from what I have been doing — if I can hit the key; rather more of a sentimental tremolo to it. It may thus help to prepare me for *Sophia*, which is to contain three ladies, and a kind of a love affair between the heroine and a dying planter who is a poet! large orders for R. L. S.

Oh, the German taboo is quite over; no soul attempts to support the C. J. or the President, they are past hope; the whites have just refused their taxes — I mean the council has refused to call for them, and if the council consented, nobody would pay; 't is a farce, and the curtain is going to fall briefly. Consequently in my History, I say as little as may be of the two dwindling stars. Poor devils! I liked the one, and the other has a little wife, now lying in! There was no man born with so little animosity as I. When I heard the C. J. was in low spirits and never left his house, I could scarce refrain from going to him.

It was a fine feeling to have finished the History; there ought to be a future state to reward that grind! It's not literature, you know; only journalism, and pedantic journalism. I had but the one desire, to get the thing as right as might be, and avoid false concords — even if that! And

it was more than there was time for.
However, there it is : done.   And if Samoa
turns up again, my book has to be counted
with, being the only narrative extant.
Milton and I — if you kindly excuse the
juxtaposition — harnessed ourselves to
strange waggons, and I at least will be
found to have plodded very soberly with
my load.   There is not even a good sentence in it, but perhaps — I don't know —
it may be found an honest, clear volume.

Wednesday.

Never got a word set down, and continues
on Thursday 19th May, his own marriage
day as ever was.   News; yes.   The C. J.
came up to call on us!   After five months'
cessation on my side, and a decidedly pain-
ful interchange of letters, I could not go
down — *could* not — to see him.   My three
ladies received him, however; he was very
agreeable as usual, but refused wine, beer,
water, lemonade, chocolate and at last a
cigarette.   Then my wife asked him, " So

you refuse to break bread?" and he waved his hands amiably in answer. All my three ladies received the same impression that he had serious matters in his mind: now we hear he is quite cock-a-hoop since the mail came, and going about as before his troubles darkened. But what did he want with me? 'T is thought he had received a despatch — and that he misreads it (so we fully believe) to the effect that they are to have war ships at command and can make their little war after all. If it be so, and they do it, it will be the meanest wanton slaughter of poor men for the salaries of two white failures. But what was his errand with me? Perhaps to warn me that unless I behave he now hopes to be able to pack me off in the *Curaçoa* when she comes.

I have celebrated my holiday from *Samoa* by a plunge at the beginning of *The Young Chevalier*. I am afraid my touch is a little broad in a love story; I can't mean one thing and write another. As for women,

I am no more in any fear of them; I can do a sort all right; age makes me less afraid of a petticoat, but I am a little in fear of grossness. However, this David Balfour's love affair, that's all right — might be read out to a mother's meeting — or a daughter's meeting. The difficulty in a love yarn, which dwells at all on love, is the dwelling on one string; it is manifold, I grant, but the root fact is there unchanged, and the sentiment being very intense, and already very much handled in letters, positively calls for a little pawing and gracing. With a writer of my prosaic literalness and pertinency of point of view, this all shoves toward grossness — positively even towards the far more damnable *closeness.* This has kept me off the sentiment hitherto, and now I am to try: Lord! Of course Meredith can do it, and so could Shakespeare; but with all my romance, I am a realist and a prosaist, and a most fanatical lover of plain physical sensations plainly and expressly rendered; hence my

perils.   To do love in the same spirit as I
did (for instance) D. Balfour's fatigue in
the heather; my dear sir, there were grossness — ready made! And hence, how to
sugar?   However, I have nearly done with
Marie-Madeleine, and am in good hopes of
Marie-Salomé, the real heroine, the other
is only a prologuial heroine to introduce
the hero.

Friday.

Anyway, the first prologuial episode is
done, and Fanny likes it.   There are only
four characters; Francis Blair of Balmile
(Jacobite Lord Gladsmuir) my hero; the
Master of Ballantrae; Paradon, a wine-
seller of Avignon; Marie-Madeleine his
wife.   These two last I am now done with,
and I think they are successful, and I hope
I have Balmile on his feet; and the style
seems to be found.   It is a little charged
and violent; sins on the side of violence;
but I think will carry the tale.   I think it
is a good idea so to introduce my hero,
being made love to by an episodic woman.

This queer tale — I mean queer for me —
has taken a great hold upon me. Where
the devil shall I go next? This is simply
the tale of a *coup de tête* of a young man
and a young woman; with a nearly, perhaps a wholly, tragic sequel, which I desire
to make thinkable right through, and sensible; to make the reader, as far as I shall
be able, eat and drink and breathe it.
Marie-Salomé des Saintes-Maries is, I
think, the heroine's name; she has got to
be yet: *sursum corda!* So has the young
Chevalier, whom I have not yet touched,
and who comes next in order. Characters:
Balmile, or Lord Gladsmuir, *comme vous
voulez;* Prince Charlie; Earl Marischal;
Master of Ballantrae; and a spy, and Dr.
Archie Campbell, and a few nondescripts;
then, of women, Marie-Salomé and Flora
Blair; seven at the outside; really four full
lengths, and I suppose a half-dozen episodic
profiles. How I must bore you with these
ineptitudes! Have patience. I am going
to bed; it is (of all hours) eleven. I have

been forced in (since I began to write to you) to blatter to Fanny on the subject of my heroine, there being two *cruces* as to her life and history: how came she alone? and how far did she go with the Chevalier? The second must answer itself when I get near enough to see. The first is a back-breaker. Yet I know there are many reasons why a *fille de famille*, romantic, adventurous, ambitious, innocent of the world, might run from her home in these days; might she not have been threatened with a convent? might there not be some Huguenot business mixed in? Here am I, far from books; if you can help me with a suggestion, I shall say God bless you. She has to be new run away from a strict family, well-justified in her own wild but honest eyes, and meeting these three men, Charles Edward, Marischal, and Balmile, through the accident of a fire at an inn. She must not run from a marriage, I think; it would bring her in the wrong frame of mind. Once I can get her, *sola*, on the

highway, all were well with my narrative.
Perpend. And help if you can.

Lafaele, long (I hope) familiar to you,
has this day received the visit of his *son*
from Tonga; and the *son* proves to be a
very pretty, attractive young daughter! I
gave all the boys kava in honour of her
arrival; along with a lean, side-whiskered
Tongan, dimly supposed to be Lafaele's
step-father; and they have been having a
good time; in the end of my verandah, I
hear Simi, my present incapable steward,
talking Tongan with the nondescript papa.
Simi, our out-door boy, burst a succession
of blood-vessels over our work, and I had
to make a position for the wreck of one of
the noblest figures of a man I ever saw. I
believe I may have mentioned the other
day how I had to put my horse to the trot,
the canter and (at last) the gallop to run
him down. In a photograph I hope to
send you (perhaps with this) you will see
Simi standing in the verandah in profile.
As a steward, one of his chief points is to

1892
May

break crystal; he is great on fracture — what do I say? — explosion! He cleans a glass, and the shards scatter like a comet's bowels.

N. B. — If I should by any chance be deported, the first of the rules hung up for that occasion is to communicate with you by telegraph. — Mind, I do not fear it, but it *is* possible.

Monday 25th.

We have had a devil of a morning of upset and bustle; the bronze candlestick Faauma has returned to the family, in time to take her position of stepmamma, and it is pretty to see how the child is at once at home, and all her terrors ended.

27th. Mail day.

And I don't know that I have much to report. I may have to leave for Malie as soon as these mail packets are made up. 'T is a necessity (if it be one) I rather deplore. I think I should have liked to lazy; but I dare say all it means is the delay of a day or so in harking back to David Balfour; that respectable youth chides at being left (where he is now) in Glasgow with the Lord Advocate, and after five years in the British Linen, who shall blame him? I was all forenoon yesterday down in Apia, dictating, and Lloyd type-writing, the conclusion of *Samoa;* and then at home correcting till the dinner bell; and in the evening again till eleven of the clock. This morning I have made up most of my packets, and I think my mail is all ready but two more, and the tag of this. I would never deny (as D. B. might say) that I was rather tired of it. But I have a damned good dose of the devil in my pipe-stem atomy; I have had my little holiday outing in my kick at *The Young Chevalier*, and I guess I can settle to *David Balfour* to-morrow or Friday like a little man. I wonder if any one had ever more energy upon so little strength? — I know there is a frost; the Samoa book can only increase that — I can't help it, that

book is not written for me but for Miss
Manners; but I mean to break that frost
inside two years, and pull off a big success,
and Vanity whispers in my ear that I have
the strength.   If I have n't, whistle ower
the lave o't!   I can do without glory, and
perhaps the time is not far off when I
can do without corn.   It is a time coming
soon enough, anyway; and I have endured
some two and forty years without public
shame, and had a good time as I did it.
If only I could secure a violent death,
what a fine success!   I wish to die in
my boots; no more Land of Counterpane
for me.   To be drowned, to be shot, to be
thrown from a horse — ay, to be hanged,
rather than pass again through that slow
dissolution.

I fancy this gloomy ramble is caused by
a twinge of age; I put on an under-shirt
yesterday (it was the only one I could find)
that barely came under my trousers; and
just below it, a fine healthy rheumatism
has now settled like a fire in my hip.

From such small causes do these valuable
considerations flow!

I shall now say adieu, dear Sir, having ten rugged miles before me and the horrors of a native feast and parliament without an interpreter, for to-day I go alone.

Yours ever,

R. L. S.

END OF VOL. I.